AN INTRODUCTORY GUIDE TO R

An Introductory Guide to R

Easing the Learning Curve

Eric L. Einspruch

THE GUILFORD PRESS
New York   London

Copyright © 2022 The Guilford Press
A Division of Guilford Publications, Inc.
370 Seventh Avenue, Suite 1200, New York, NY 10001
www.guilford.com

Printed in the United States of America

This book is printed on acid-free paper.

Last digit is print number: 9   8   7   6   5   4   3   2   1

Library of Congress Cataloging-in-Publication Data is available from the
publisher.

ISBN: 978-1-4625-4989-4 (hardcover)
ISBN: 978-1-4625-4988-7 (paperback)

Acknowledgments

I am grateful to everyone who has in some way contributed to this book. In particular, I very much appreciate the interest, support, and insights of C. Deborah Laughton, Publisher, Methodology and Statistics, and Senior Editor, Developmental Psychology and Geography, at The Guilford Press. It has been delightful to work together again.

I want to express my gratitude to Steven R. Terrell, Nova Southeastern University, and Andrew F. Hayes, University of Calgary, for granting permission to use examples from their work. In addition, I want to thank the reviewers who provided helpful comments on the draft manuscript: Darlene Russ-Eft, Emeritus, College of Education, Oregon State University; Charlotte Tate, Department of Psychology, San Francisco State University; Michele Parker, Department of Educational Leadership, University of North Carolina, Wilmington; Julie Combs, Department of Educational Leadership, Sam Houston State University; Katerina M. Marcoulides, Psychology, University of Minnesota; and Sierra A. Bainter, Psychology, University of Miami. I also thank the R Foundation and RStudio for allowing use of images and output from R and RStudio.

I remain ever grateful to family members, friends, colleagues, and students who have supported my interests and contributed to my education across the years.

Contents

AN INTRODUCTORY GUIDE TO R

CHAPTER 1

Introduction

▽ CHAPTER OBJECTIVES

▽ State the purpose of this book.

▽ Note what you will be able to do after reading this book.

▽ Say whom the book is for.

▽ Describe the book's approach.

W elcome, dear reader, to the amazing world of R!

Purpose of This Book

The R statistical analysis software (R Core Team, 2021), a remarkably powerful tool for statistical analysis, has enjoyed considerable growth in popularity in a variety of industries. RStudio (*https://rstudio.com*), an integrated development environment (IDE), is popular among R users.[1]

---

[1]An IDE is an application that combines activities that are common when writing computer code, easing the code writing task, and thereby improving efficiency and productivity. The RStudio IDE includes a Console; a syntax-highlighting editor that supports code completion, smart indentation, and the ability to directly execute code; integrated R help and documentation; a workspace browser and data viewer; and debugging, authoring, and other tools.

The R statistical analysis software provides powerful data analysis tools for researchers, program evaluators, and others who cannot afford (or who do not want to spend money on) the cost of other analytic software.

However, R has a steep learning curve, especially for those who have only ever used pull-down menus (rather than writing analytic syntax) to analyze data and who therefore may be concerned about the prospect of learning the software. R's remarkable functionality and flexibility contribute to this difficulty, as an analytic task often may be successfully accomplished in several different ways using the R software. As a result, users who are new to R encounter a bewildering collection of possibilities, sometimes with little or no guidance about which path to take. The purpose of this book is to overcome this difficulty by providing a clear, concise, and direct path to learning R.

What You Will Be Able to Do after Reading This Book

This book introduces the use of R to conduct fundamental data analysis tasks, including working within the RStudio IDE, reading data, data wrangling, data analysis, data visualization, and reporting in a manner that supports reproducible research. The book will be particularly helpful for those who are just getting started using R. After working through this book, you will be able to:

1. Use R to accomplish fundamental data handling, analysis, visualization, and reporting tasks, and
2. Know how to find and use additional resources to further your R capabilities.

I have written this book in a friendly manner to facilitate ease of access to the material, with an emphasis on learning how to learn to use R. The book will be of value to anyone who wants gentle guidance into the amazing world of R. Rest assured, you *can* learn and use this software, and it can even be fun.

Whom This Book Is For

I have written this book to be accessible by anyone who has a basic understanding of how to handle data analysis tasks. The book assumes no prior familiarity with R, and it is written particularly for those who are timid about learning R. The book introduces the use of R for a variety of statistical procedures, but it does not teach the procedures themselves. Thus, I assume that readers either already have an understanding of basic statistics or are simultaneously learning basic statistics elsewhere (and this book will certainly support you in the process of learning statistics).

Data analysis software is used in pretty much every field that conducts quantitative research. Thus, this book has a broad general audience. More specifically, it is intended for anyone who wants an efficient, direct, and gentle introduction to using R. The book supports those with limited resources by helping overcome the steep learning curve for this free software, thus helping to make it easily accessible to a wide variety of users.

This book can be used in an undergraduate or graduate course on analytic methods, as either a primary or supplemental text, depending on course coverage. The book can also be used to support training in workshop or other formats. Those who are learning R on their own will also find the book useful.

Approach

Using R to solve data analysis puzzles can be quite interesting, and my goal is to ease the learning curve for R by providing a user-friendly introduction to the software. My philosophy is also that learning can be fun and that by thinking about the process of becoming familiar with R, readers are empowered to further their learning beyond this book and into the vast domain of R's remarkable resources. I emphasize a direct approach to helping you learn how to use R to accomplish fundamental data analysis tasks. This differs from approaches that emphasize R itself and its many options, rather than analysis tasks immediately at hand. The text is supported by example code, screenshots, and output from analyses.

This book also emphasizes good work habits and processes that make tracking one's work easier. (For example, comments within the R code can be used to document decisions made in the process of carrying out a project and its related data analysis.) This emphasis supports research reproducibility, which is largely a matter of policy and good work habits. This is particularly important for those who wish to reproduce a previous study's results as a prelude to secondary analyses or for those who wish to replicate a study at a new time, in a new geographic location, or with a new population.

The book begins with instructions on downloading and installing R and RStudio. It then continues with an overview of RStudio and how to download and install R packages, which add functionality to the initial Base R installation. Packages include code, documentation, and other information that can be shared among users and provide tools for accomplishing tasks in R. Packages support reproducibility through sharing code that users develop to solve data handling and analysis problems (an advantage of R is that we, too, can develop and share our own packages if we are interested in doing so). From there, the book introduces the use of R for data handling, analysis, visualization, and reporting. This content describes both *Base R* and *Tidyverse* approaches to working in R. It will help you develop a sense for both because some capabilities are available using one approach but not the other, and also because you may need to work with people who adopt one or the other approach. Finally, the book briefly introduces user-written functions and offers ideas about next steps in learning R.

Keep in mind throughout this book that you *can* learn R. As is true about learning anything new, especially a new language, it will take time and practice. As you work through the book, be sure to enter and run the R code, so that you take a hands-on approach to actively engage with the material. Be gentle, remember to breathe, take a break whenever you need one (especially if you find yourself stuck or frustrated), and have some fun. Let's go!

KEY TAKEAWAYS

- R is a powerful tool for statistical analysis that is also free.

- The purpose of this book is to provide a clear, concise, and direct path to learning R and to help you learn how to learn more about using R.

- After reading this book you will be able to:

  - Use R for fundamental data handling, analysis, visualization, and reporting, and

  - Know to find and use additional resources to further your R capabilities.

- It is important to be able to work from both Base R and Tidyverse approaches.

- The book is written in a friendly manner to facilitate ease of access to the material.

- You *can* learn and use R software, and it *can* be fun.

Getting Started

▼ Download and install R.

▼ Download and install RStudio.

▼ Become familiar with RStudio fundamentals.

▼ Read data into R.

▼ Write (save) data from R.

▼ Muse on debugging R code.

The first step in working with R is obtaining the necessary software. This includes R itself and, to make it easier to use, the RStudio integrated development environment (IDE). The first section of this chapter will show you how to:

- Download and install R,
- Work directly in the R Console,
- Download and install RStudio, and
- Begin working in RStudio.

The second section of this chapter will introduce RStudio fundamentals and help you understand:

- RStudio window panes,
- Some ways to customize RStudio,

- RStudio projects, and
- How to download and install R Packages.

In the third section of this chapter, we will:

- Read data into R,
- View data,
- Write (save) data,
- Enter data into R via inline code, and
- Muse on debugging R code.

Download and Install R

R is housed on the Comprehensive R Archive Network (CRAN) website (as are R packages). You can follow these steps to download and install R.

Windows Users

1. Go to the CRAN website: *https://cran.r-project.org.*
2. In the *Download and Install R* box in the upper center of the page, click on the *Download R for Windows* link.
3. On the next page, click on the *install R for the first time* link.
4. On the next page, click on the *Download R x.x.x for Windows* link (where x.x.x is the current version of R).
5. Double-click on the downloaded file to run the installation.

Mac Users

1. Go to the CRAN website: *https://cran.r-project.org.*
2. In the *Download and Install R* box in the upper center of the page, click on *Download R for (Mac) OS X* link.
3. On the next page, click on the *R-x.x.x.pkg* link (where x.x.x is the current version of R).
4. Install the downloaded file.

Work Directly in the R Console

Working directly in the R Console is possible, although it is quite limiting, so we will only look at a brief example of how that is done and then promptly move on to working in RStudio. Nevertheless, working directly in the R Console is useful as an introduction to R. To start, launch R on your computer by double-clicking on the shortcut that was created during installation, and you will see the R Console shown in Figure 2.1 (or similar, depending on your computer's operating system).[1] At the command prompt in the R Console (the ">"), type *2 + 2* as shown in Figure 2.2. Finally, press your computer's "Enter" key to see the result, as displayed in Figure 2.3.

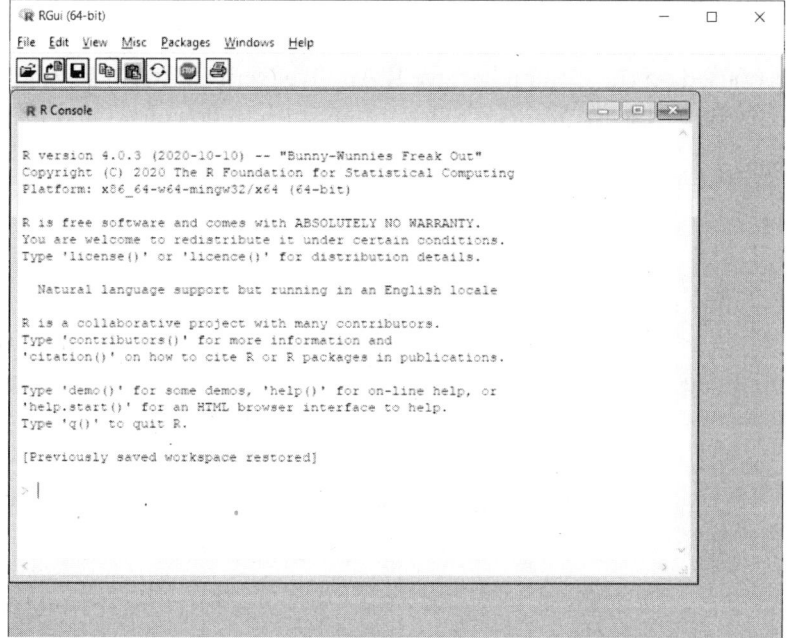

FIGURE 2.1. The R Console.

---

[1] If you do not have a shortcut for some reason (for example, if you deleted it), you can launch R from the Windows search bar by searching for the filename "Rgui.exe" or by double-clicking on that file using File Explorer. You can also re-create the shortcut (the filepath for the version that is current at the time of this writing is C:\Program Files\R\R-4.0.3\bin\x64\Rgui.exe).

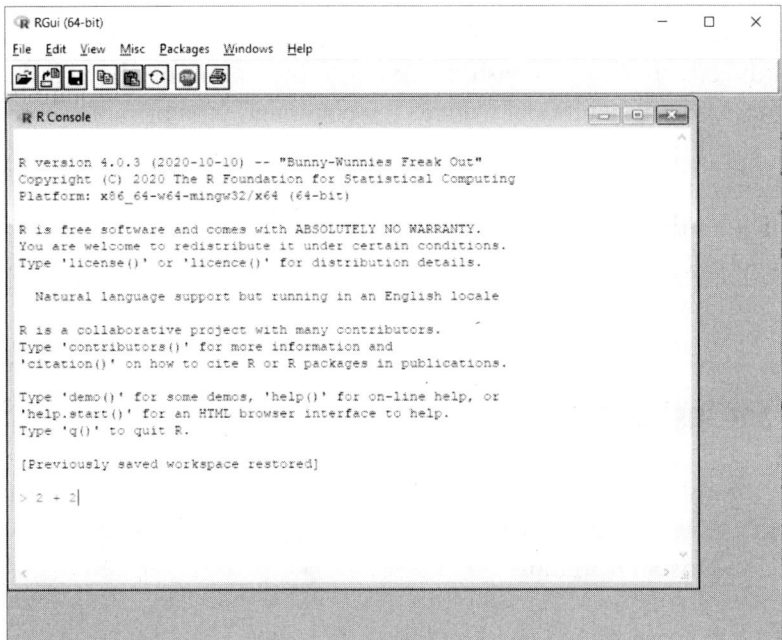

FIGURE 2.2. The R Console with a command waiting to be entered.

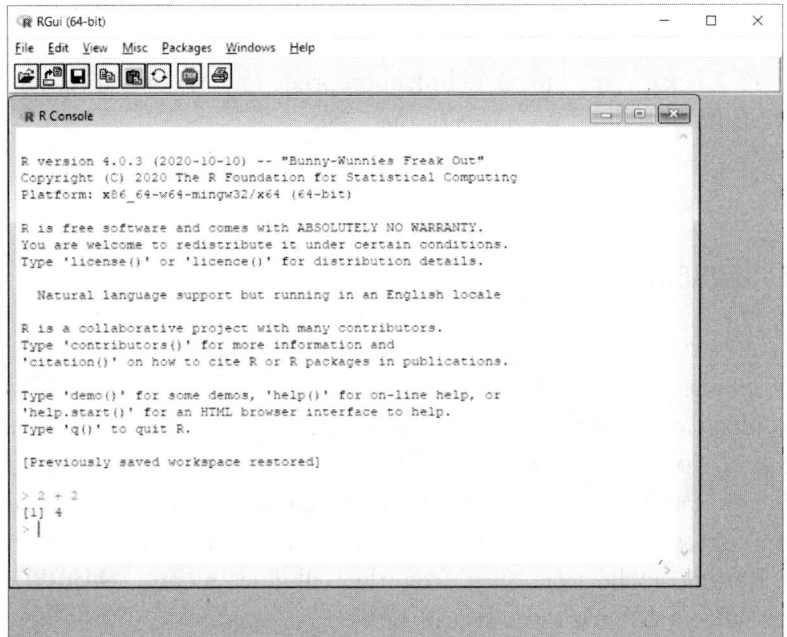

FIGURE 2.3. The R Console with the result from the command in Figure 2.2.

You have now successfully used R! You can further explore working directly in R as you wish, for example by examining the pull-down menus or doing additional work at the command prompt (note that you can scroll through previous commands using the up and down arrows). When you are ready, you can end your R session by either using **File →** **Exit** from the pull-down menus or by entering **quit()** at the command prompt). R will show the dialog box with the question *Save workspace image?*, to which you may answer *No*.

Download and Install RStudio

RStudio is a remarkable IDE with a great deal of functionality, which greatly eases working with R. You can take the following steps to download and install RStudio.

1. Go to the RStudio website: *https://rstudio.com*.
2. Click on *Download* in the upper right-hand corner (or elsewhere if it has moved).
3. Choose your version—for our purposes, choose the free version of *RStudio Desktop*.
4. Click on the download link appropriate for your operating system (for example, Windows or macOS).
5. Double-click on the downloaded file to run the installation.

RStudio Fundamentals

In this section you will gain basic familiarity with RStudio and related workflow concepts that help make work more efficient. You will also download and install R packages, which enhance Base R's functionality. To start working in RStudio, first launch the program from your computer by double-clicking on the shortcut that was created during installation, or by entering *RStudio* in the Windows search bar and selecting the RStudio application. Next, from the pull-down menus, select **File →** **New File → R Script** (see Figure 2.4).

We write our code in an R script, and we run the code from within the script, similarly to the way we write and run code, which other

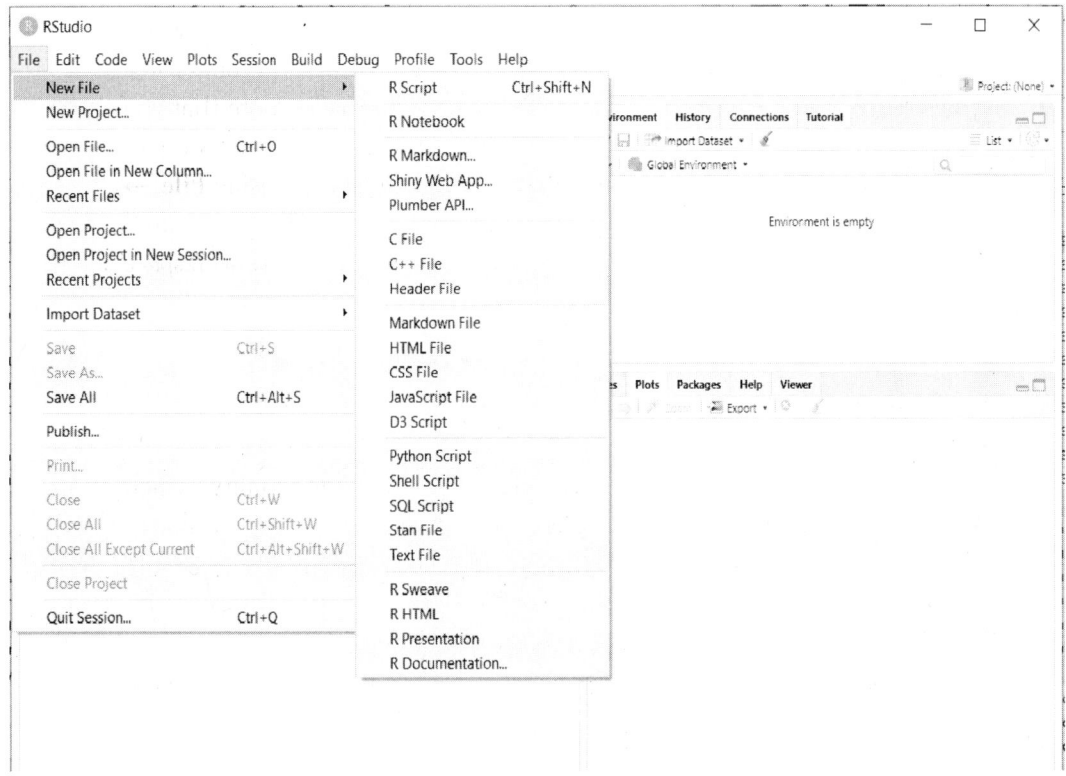

FIGURE 2.4. Opening a new script in RStudio.

analysis software programs might refer to as *syntax*. This approach has clear advantages over analyzing data using pull-down menus in that it gives full access to the tools available in the software, allows documentation of the code using comments, makes it easier to rerun analyses, reduces the potential for inconsistency when rerunning analyses, and makes it easier to share code among users. These advantages make learning to write and run code, rather than relying on pull-down menus to conduct analyses, well worth the effort.

RStudio Panes

Your computer screen now looks like the image in Figure 2.5 (or similar to it, depending on your operating system and the default settings for how RStudio launched).

FIGURE 2.5. RStudio with four panes open.

Notice that RStudio has four panes. The upper left-hand pane is where we write and run R code. The upper right-hand pane provides access to the session environment and history. The lower right-hand pane provides access to files, plots, packages, and help. The lower left-hand pane provides access to the Console and terminal. This is the same Console that we saw when working directly in R. To see this in action, at the command prompt in the RStudio Console, type *2 + 2* and then press enter. The result will appear in the Console, as before when working directly in R (see Figure 2.6). To end your RStudio Session, from the pull-down menus select **File → Quit Session . . .** (If you are prompted by a dialog box with the question *Save workspace image?*, you may answer *No*.).

Congratulations! You have now downloaded and installed R and RStudio, worked directly in R using the R Console, and made the transition to RStudio by getting an overview of the RStudio window and by finding and using the R Console within RStudio.

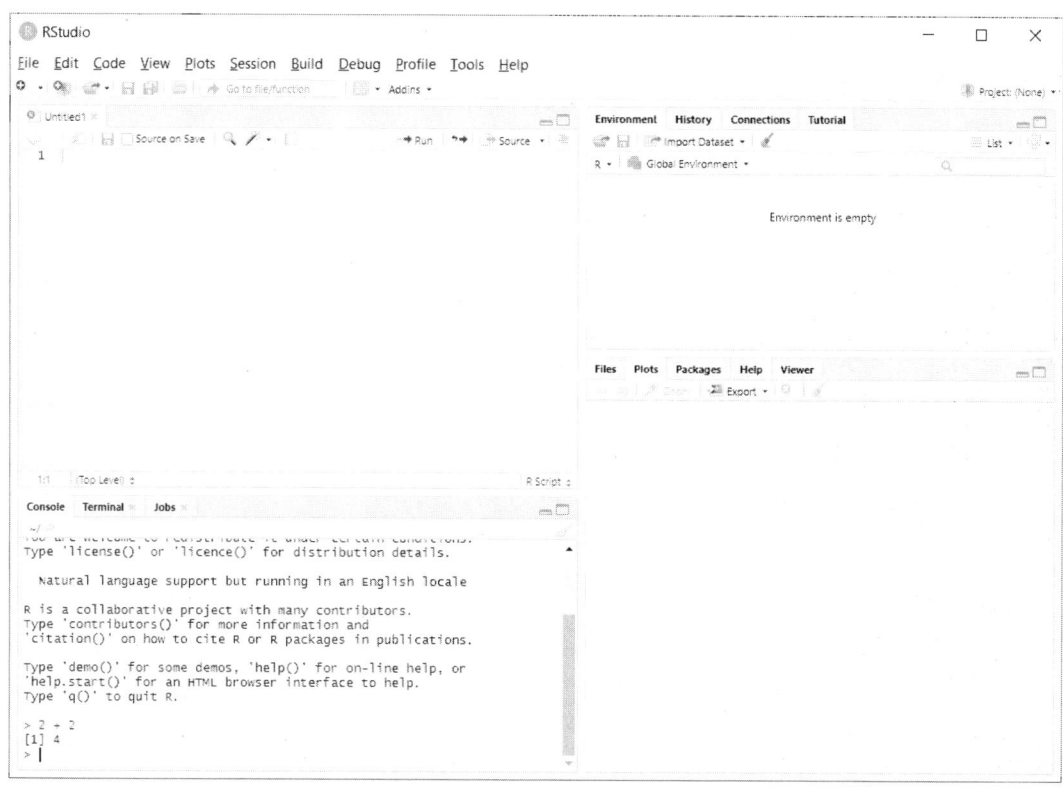

FIGURE 2.6. Working in the RStudio Console.

Customizing RStudio

RStudio offers many options for customizing how you work in the IDE, which are accessed through the **Tools** pull-down menu. General options related to working in RStudio are available by selecting **Tools → Global Options . . .** Options related to working on particular RStudio projects are available by selecting **Tools → Project Options . . .** As one example, I recommend that you do not save the R workspace[2] when you exit RStudio (but do save your work before exiting!!), so as to rely on your R scripts rather than on the environment for your code. To make RStudio automatically not save your R workspace between sessions, select **Tools → Global Options . . .** , and you will see the dialog box in Figure 2.7. Under the *Workspace* options, uncheck the checkbox next to *Restore*

---

[2]The current environment, including the objects stored in it, is called the *workspace*.

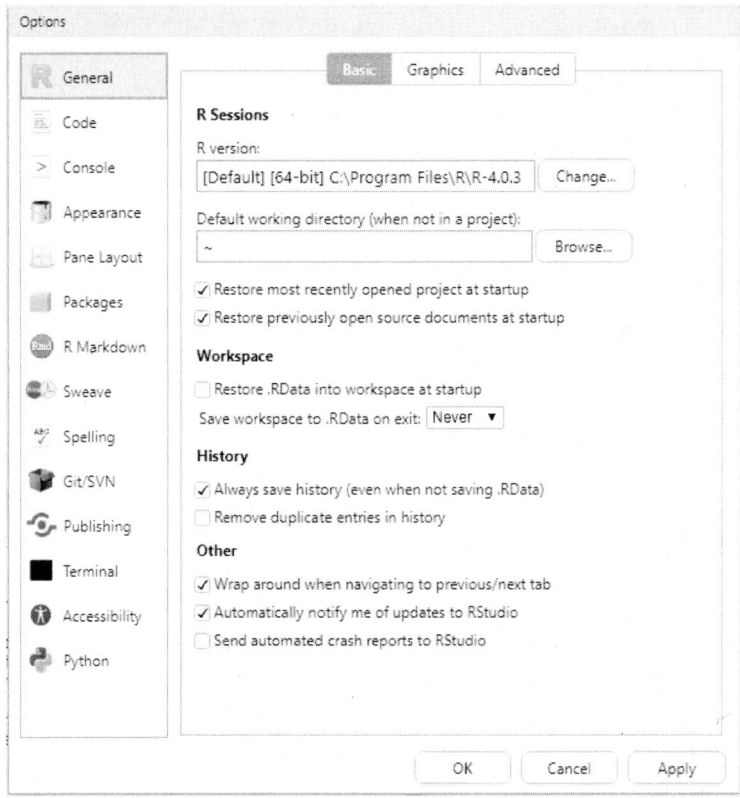

FIGURE 2.7. RStudio Global Options dialog box.

.RData into workspace at startup, and set the *Save workspace to .RData on exit:* to the *Never* option. Then click the *Apply* button to apply the new settings (you will need to restart RStudio for it to apply the new settings).

RStudio Projects

I strongly encourage you to keep all your files (for example, data, analysis code, and output) for any particular project together in an *R Project*. This is easy to do using RStudio. You can create a project for use with this book as follows. First, select **File → New Project . . .** and you will see the dialog box in Figure 2.8.

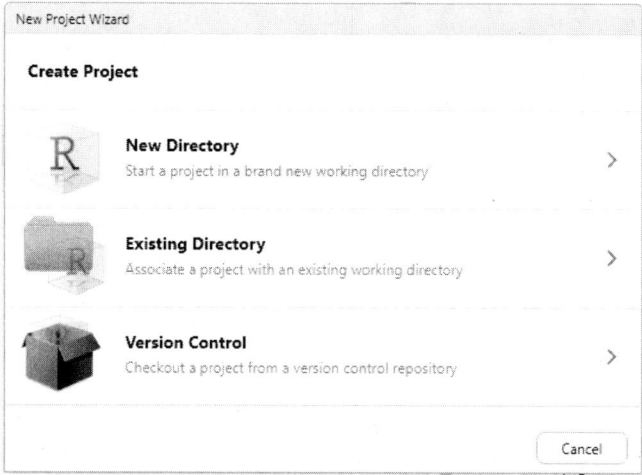

FIGURE 2.8. Create Project dialog box.

Select *New Directory* to create a new directory for the project, and you will see the *New Project, Project Type* dialog box in Figure 2.9.

Select *New Project* and you will see the *New Project, Create New Project* dialog box in Figure 2.10. In the dialog box, enter "Introductory Guide to R" for the directory name, then click the *Browse* button and navigate to whichever directory you would like the new directory to be a

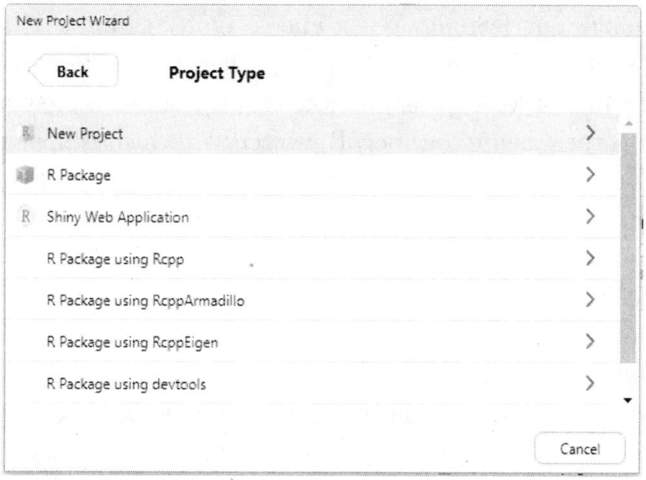

FIGURE 2.9. New Project, Project Type dialog box.

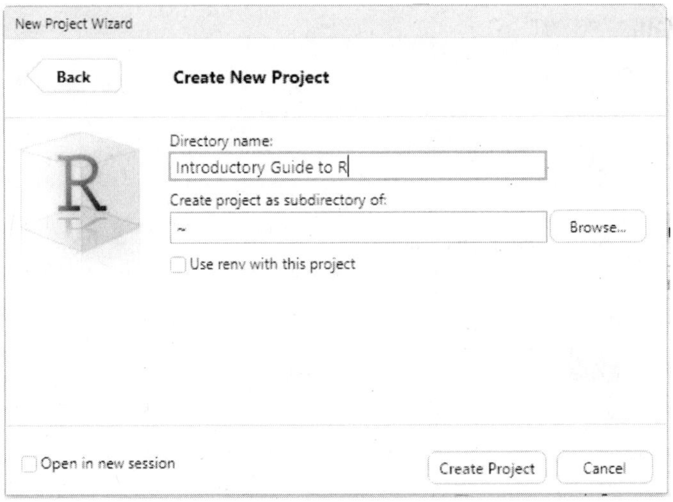

FIGURE 2.10. New Project, Create New Project dialog box.

subdirectory of (in Figure 2.10 you see that I navigated to the *Documents* directory, hence the tilde ["~"] in the figure).

Now click the *Create Project* button and your new project will open in RStudio. Notice that the project name ("Introductory Guide to R") now appears in the project button in the upper right-hand corner of RStudio.

If you now quit RStudio (select **File → Quit Session . . .**) and then examine your folders, you will see that the new folder has been created. If you look in that folder, you will note that RStudio has created several files, one of them being your new R project file (which is named "Introductory Guide to R" and is of the type "R Project"). If you double-click on the project file, it will open in RStudio. You can also open the project from within RStudio by first launching RStudio, then selecting **File → Open Project . . .** and navigating to your project to open it. Once your project is open in RStudio, you will see the project name in the upper left-hand corner of RStudio and in the Project pull-down menu in the upper right-hand corner of RStudio (from which you can create a new project, open an existing project, close a project, and access project options). In the lower right-hand pane, you will see your files listed in the **File** tab.

Download, Install, and Load R Packages

Base R, which you installed when you installed R, has considerable capabilities. However, R's capabilities can be vastly expanded by downloading and installing modules known as *Packages*. Packages include R code, sample data, and documentation. Packages are stored in a *library* on your computer. Packages only need to be downloaded once (although updates may become available), but they need to be loaded each time you begin an R session (but only once per session).

Among the packages we will use in this book are those included in what is known as the Tidyverse (*www.tidyverse.org*). The Tidyverse is a collection of packages that are designed to work together by sharing an underlying design philosophy, grammar, and data structures. Working in the Tidyverse may be more intuitive than working in Base R (for example, the way code is written using what is known as the *pipe*, as we will see in the next chapter), and it may also be easier in that the Tidyverse packages work together given their shared underlying concepts. However, there are times we may want to use tools that are included in packages written for Base R rather than the Tidyverse, or we may be working in a setting that is oriented toward Base R. We will look at the concept of *tidy data* later in this book.

To install R packages using RStudio, select **Tools → Install Packages . . .** to open the *Install Packages* dialog box. Then enter the name of the package you want to install. You can install the entire collection of Tidyverse packages simply by entering *tidyverse* into the *Packges (separate multiple with space or comma):* line in the dialog box. Install the packages from *Repository CRAN*, and install them to your default library (see Figure 2.11; note that in the figure I have deleted the library pathname since the pathname for my library will be different from the one for your library). You will also want to install the package dependencies, so be sure that the box is checked. Click on the *Install* button and RStudio will install the collection of Tidyverse packages (be patient, as this may take a few minutes).

To load a package into your RStudio session, simply type **library(*name*)** in the Script window and then press Ctrl+Enter to run that line of code. Let's load the collection of Tidyverse packages by typing *library(tidyverse)* in the Script window and then running that line of

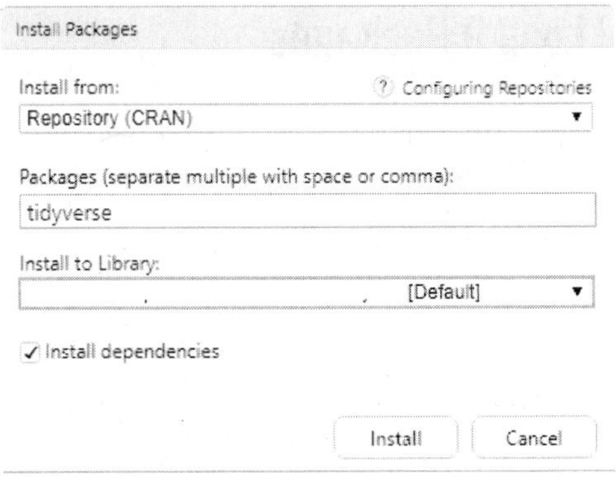

FIGURE 2.11. Install Packages dialog box.

FIGURE 2.12. Loading the Tidyverse collection of packages.

code (see Figure 2.12). Keep in mind that **R is case sensitive** and you must therefore use a lower-case "t" in this line of code; running a line of code that says *library(Tidyverse)* will result in an error message saying that there is no package called Tidyverse.

Read Data into R

While it is possible to enter data directly into R using inline code (more about this later), it is more convenient to enter your data elsewhere (for example, in an Excel file) and then read it into R. You can also read data files that were saved using other statistical software (for example, SPSS or SAS data files) into R. In this section we will read data into R and then look at the raw data.

Use Comments to Document R Code

It is important to use comments to document your R code. Comments can provide reminders about the purpose of different parts of the code, and they can also document decisions that were made about how a project was conducted or about how the data were cleaned and analyzed. This will be helpful when you return to the code at a later date or when you pass the code along to another person. If you write your code cryptically, with little or no documentation, you (or someone else) will end up spending time in the future trying to figure out what the code does and why it does it. Thus, comments are an important part of reproducible research (that is, someone with access to your data and analytic code could exactly reproduce your results).

We use the " # " symbol in R to begin a comment. Text following the " # " until the end of that line will be ignored by R. Comments may start at the beginning of the line (as in most comments in this book), but they may also occur in a line following other code.

The Assignment Operator in R

We use the assignment operator " <- " to create objects in R. For example, in just a moment we will use an R function to read data from Excel and assign it to an R object that will be our data set. This will be clear once you work through the example. In RStudio, you can type " <- " from the keyboard, or you can use the **Alt + minus sign** as a keyboard shortcut.

Read Data from Excel

Let's first create an Excel file called *Patient_Data* in the *Introductory Guide to R* folder on your computer (see Table 2.1), which contains the data in Figure 2.1.

Let's now read this data file into RStudio. First, enter the following code into your R Script. Substitute your name for "[Name]" and the current date for "[Date]." Then use either **File → Save As . . .** or **Ctrl + S** or the **file save icon** in the upper left-hand corner of RStudio to save the file, giving it the name *Read Patient Data*. Also, know that many other options are available for reading Excel files—for example, specifying which sheet to read, and directly stating whether the first row in the spreadsheet is a header.

TABLE 2.1. Patient Data

Gender	Health perception	Anxiety	Exercise (minutes)
F	3	100	0
M	2	55	60
F	1	80	10
F	1	25	45
F	2	65	30
M	3	90	15
M	3	100	45
F	1	40	50
F	2	10	40
F	2	0	60

Note. From Terrell (2021, p. 51).

```
#
# Read data from Excel
#
#
# By [Name]
# [Date]

# Load packages
library(tidyverse)
library(readxl)

# Read Patient Data
patient_data <- read_excel("Patient_Data.xlsx")
```

This script:

- Provides comments using the "#" symbol.
- Loads the Tidyverse collection of core packages.
- Loads the *readxl* package (this package must be loaded explicitly, since it is not a core package loaded by the *library(tidyverse)* line.
- Uses the *read_excel()* function to read an Excel file (we can specify which sheet to read either by name or order, for example, if we want to read the second sheet in an Excel file that is named *Sheet 2*, then we can use *read_excel(Patient_Data.xlsx, 2)* or *read_excel(Patient_Data.xlsx, "Sheet 2")*.
- Uses the assignment operator "<–" to assign the results of the function to an object, in this case a *data frame* (a kind of data structure in R) called *patient_data*.

We can name things in R using snake_case, camelCase, or periods. in.names. For example, we could give the data frame we just created the name *patientdata*, *patient_data*, *patientData*, or *patient.data*. Those names are all OK, and we can choose an approach based on preference, workplace convention, or some other reason. Regardless of the chosen approach, I encourage you to be consistent, at least within any one R script. Style guidance may be found in the Tidyverse Style Guide (*https://style.tidyverse.org*).

Now run this script by selecting all the lines of code and pressing **Ctrl + Enter** or the **Run** button in the upper right-hand corner of the

FIGURE 2.13. RStudio after reading the patient data.

Script pane or by selecting **Code → Run Selected Line(s)**. Your RStudio window will then look like Figure 2.13.

Let's take a look at our RStudio session at this point. In the Scripts pane, we have the code that we just wrote. In the Environment pane, we have the data frame that was just created, called *patient_data*, which has 10 observations and 4 variables (if it doesn't, check that your Excel file matches Table 2.1, correct any errors, and then rerun your R script). The files pane now has four files, including your project file, your script, and your Excel file. Finally, the Console pane lists the lines of code that you just ran.

Note Regarding Pathnames in R

If in your script you want to point to a file that is not in your current working directory (for example, not in your project directory), you will need to specify the full pathname as well as the filename. In doing so, R uses the forward slash (" / ") rather than the backslash (" \ ") that is used in the Windows environment.

Look at the Data

There are several ways that we can take a look at the data in our dataframe.

• We can run one line of code in the Script window that contains the *view()* function and the name of the object we wish to view enclosed in parentheses: *view(patient_data)*. This opens a tab in the upper left-hand pane that lets us view the data (see Figure 2.14). Although this tab has the appearance of a spreadsheet, it is not a spreadsheet and so we cannot edit the data in the tab.

• We can run one line of code in the Script window that simply contains the name of the object we wish to see the contents of, in this case the dataframe named *patient_data*. The result of running that line of code (which only contains one word: *patient_data*) will appear in the

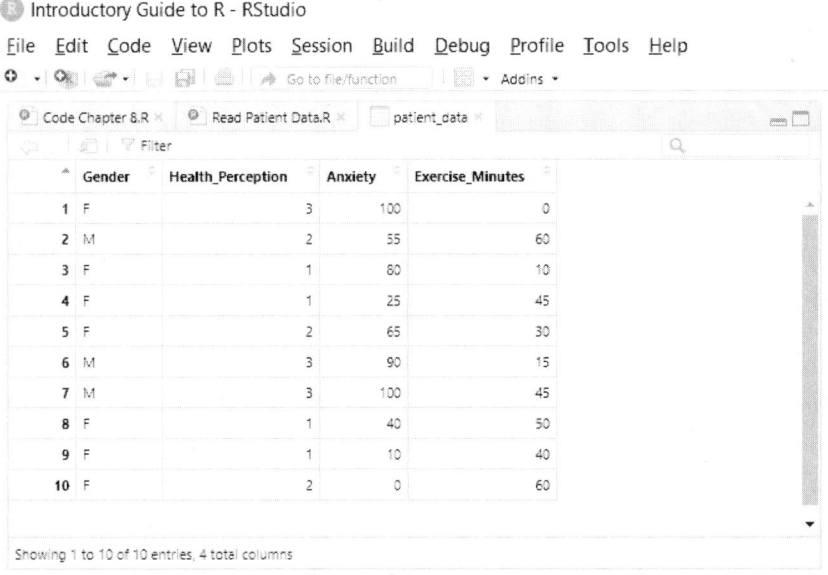

FIGURE 2.14. Tab showing view of data.

Console pane. There we will see that the object is a *tilbble* (a kind of data frame that is part of the Tidyverse[3]) with 10 rows and 4 variables, the type of each variable,[4] and a listing of the first rows of the dataframe.

- We can run one line of code in the Script window that contains the *print()* function and the name of the object we wish to view enclosed in parentheses: *print(patient_data)*. This prints several lines of the data in the Console. We can also use "*n = [number]*" to specify the number of lines to print. For example, *print(patient_data, n = 20)* prints the first 20 lines of the data, and *print(patient_data, n = Inf)* prints all of the lines of the data.

- Similar to the *print()* function, we can use the *head()* function to print the first lines of the data, and we can use the *tail()* function to print the last lines of the data. We can also use the *slice()* function to print a certain row(s) of the data. For example, *slice(patient_data, 3)* prints the third row of the data, and *slice(patient_data, 3:8)* prints rows 3 through 8 of the data.

Read Data in Other Formats

R can read data from a variety of other formats. In this section, we will look at reading data from comma-separated values (CSV) files, and then look at using the *haven* package for reading SPSS, SAS, and Stata data files.

Read Data from a CSV File

You can use the *read_csv()* function to read a CSV file. If the file has a header row with variable names, use the *header = TRUE* option. The following code uses the *read_csv()* function to read a CSV file (that has a header) and assigns the results of the function to an object called *dataframe*:

---

[3] Tibbles have some printing and subsetting features that differ from classic Base R dataframes.

[4] In this example, gender is a *character* variable, and the other three variables are *doubles*, a type of numeric variable.

```
# Read a CSV file
#
# If the file has a header row with the names of the variables:
data_frame <- read_csv("filename.csv", header = TRUE)
#
# If the file does not have a header row with
# the names of the variables:
data_frame <- read_csv("filename.csv")
```

Read Data from an SPSS, SAS, or Stata File

The *haven* package is part of the Tidyverse and can be used to read SPSS, SAS, or Stata files. Remember to load the package into your session before trying to use it:

```
# Load the haven package
library(haven)
```

Once the package is loaded, you can use the appropriate function to read the file type you are working with. The following code uses different functions within the *haven* package to read their associated file types and assigns the results of the function to an object called *data_frame*:

```
# Read an SPSS data file
data_frame <- read_sav("filename.sav")

# Read a SAS data file
data_frame <- read_sas("filename.sas7bdat")

# Read a SAS data file with an associated format file
data_frame <- read_sas("datafilename.sas7bdat", "formatfilename")

# Read a Stata file
data_frame <- read_dta("filename.dta")
```

Read Data from an R Data File

R has its own format for data files called RDS. The following code uses the *read_rds()* function to read a RDS file and assigns the results of the function to an object called *data_frame*:

```
# Read an R data file (RDS)
data_frame <- read_rds("filename.rds")
```

Write Data Files

If you want to save your data files as you work through your analyses, for efficiency I suggest that you save them in the RDS format. However, you can also write data files in other formats. The general format for this code is: *function(name of the data frame to be written, "file name")*

Here are some examples:

```
# Write an R data file (RDS)
write_rds(dataframe, "filename")

# Write a CSV data file
write_csv(dataframe, "filename")

# Write an SPSS data file
write_sav(dataframe, "filename")

# Write a SAS data file
write_sas(dataframe, "filename")

# Write a Stata data file
write_dta(dataframe, "filename")
```

Entering Data via Inline Code

You can enter data directly in your script file if you have a need to (for example, you may wish to do this for a small data file). To do so, we use the Base R *concatenate* function (also referred to as the *combine* function), *c()*, which groups things together. Let's write the code that would create the *Patient Data* data frame (but change the data frame and variable names slightly to distinguish this data frame from the previous one):

```
# Create the gender variable
Gender2 <- c("F", "M", "F", "F", "F", "M", "M", "F", "F", "F")

# Create the systolic blood pressure variable
SystolicBP2 <- c(180, 175, 160, 158, 135, 135, 132, 120, 105, 90)

# Create the anxiety variable
Anxiety2 <- c(100, 55, 80, 25, 65, 90, 100, 40, 10, 0)

# Create the exercise (minutes) variable
ExerciseMin2 <- c(0,60,10,45,30,15,45,50,40,60)
```

```
# Create the data frame using the data.frame function
dataframe2 <- data.frame(Gender2, SystolicBP2, Anxiety2, ExerciseMin2)

# View the data frame in the console
dataframe2

# View the data frame in a tab
view(dataframe2)
```

Notice that as you run this code, the code you have run appears in the Console pane (along with error messages if there are any) in the lower left-hand part of RStudio, Note too that the objects you have created appear in the Environment tab in the upper right-hand part of RStudio.

Cleaning Variable Names

The *janitor* package includes the *clean_names()* function, which can be very helpful when reading in data, especially when the imported variable names are quite messy. The resulting names are unique and consist of only the underscore (" _ ") character, numbers, and letters. It is a good idea to run the *clean_names()* function whenever your read data. The following runs this function to clean the names in the *patient_data* data frame:

```
# Clean names
library(janitor)
clean_names(patient_data)
```

We run this code and then view the data frame again, comparing the new variable names to the original ones.

Clearing the Console

Sometimes after working on a chunk of R code in order to get it working the way you want it to, it is nice to run it so that it appears on its own in the Console, without the distraction of previous efforts. We can clear the Console from the pull-down menus simply by selecting **Edit → Clear Console**.

Clearing the Environment

As noted earlier, the current environment, including the objects stored in it, is called the R workspace. These objects can be displayed in the Environment tab in either *list* or *grid* format, and we can switch between these two formats using the pull-down menu in the upper right corner of the Environment tab. At some point during an R session, we may want to remove from the environment objects that are no longer needed. If we want to remove all the objects in the workspace, we can do so by selecting **Session → Clear Workspace . . .** and clicking **Yes** in the *Confirm Remove Objects* dialog box, or by clicking the *broom* icon in the Environment tab if the objects are shown in *list* format. Alternatively, we can remove the object by selecting all the objects if they are shown in *grid* format and then clicking the *broom* icon in the Environment tab (in grid format, clicking the box next to the column heading *Name* will select all of the objects). If we want to remove only certain objects, we can show them in *grid* format, select them individually, and then click the *broom* icon in the Environment tab.

Some Thoughts on Debugging R Code

R programs are rarely written so well that they are error-free the first time they are run. It is much more likely that your program will contain an error(s). Don't worry about this! Just use the error messages as a guide to figuring out the problem. RStudio also provides clues in the Script tab that are helpful in figuring out the problem. Often, the problem is just a typographic error, a mismatched number of open and closed parentheses, having used the wrong case (remember, R is case sensitive), or some similar problem. At other times, though, there is a syntax error that requires more effort to puzzle through and resolve. Consider these examples:

If we run the code

```
patient_data <- Read_excel("Patient_Data.xlsx")
```

we receive the error message

```
Error in Read_excel("Patient_Data.xlsx") :
could not find function "Read_excel"
```

That is because the *Read_excel()* function does not exist. However, the *read_excel()* function does exist, and that is the one we want. The solution is to correct our code so that it calls the *read_excel()* function rather than attempts to call the nonexistent *Read_excel()* function. Remember, R is case sensitive.

If we run the code

```
patient_data <- read_excel("Patient_Data.xlsx")
```

but we have named our data file *Patient Data.xlsx*, then we receive the error message

```
Error: `path` does not exist: 'Patient_Data.xlsx'
```

The problem is that we tried to read a file that does not exist, even though perhaps we think it does. The solution is to compare the name of the file we tried to read with the name of the file we actually have, and then correct the code so that it refers to the correct filename (or to change the filename if we want it to be what is referred to in the code). In this example, we need to either remove the underscore in the filename referenced in the code or add it to the actual filename).

If we run the code

```
patient_data <- read_excel("Patient Data.xlsx"))
```

we receive the error message

```
Error: unexpected ')' in "patient_data <-
read_excel("Patient Data.xlsx"))"
```

The problem is that we have one too many closed parentheses in the line (that is, here we have one open parenthesis and two closed parentheses), and the solution is to delete one of the two closed parentheses.

If we run the code

```
patient_data <- read_excel(("Patient Data.xlsx")
```

then RStudio pauses, and we see a plus sign (" + ") as the prompt in the Console. We also see a red circle with an " x " in it to the left of the RStudio line number of this line of code in the Script tab, as well as a red squiggly line under the first open parentheses in the line of code. If we hover over either the red circle or the red squiggly line, we see the error message

```
unmatched opening bracket '('
```

The solution is to click in the Console next to the plus sign prompt and press the escape key on the keyboard to return to the greater than sign prompt, and then remove one of the two opening parentheses.

A wealth of information is available in R, and on the Internet, that is very useful in figuring out what needs to be corrected in the code. In addition, using an error message (or our intended task, such as reading data from an Excel file) as a search term may yield the information we are looking for, or at least some clues about how to approach figuring out a coding error (see Chapter 9, for more information about this). If there are several errors in a program, it is best to correct the ones that occur first, as an early error may have caused subsequent errors, and all that is needed is to correct the earlier one(s). Once you have made your correction(s), run the program again. If it still doesn't work, then at least some of the errors have been corrected, and you just need to correct the remaining ones. *Debugging* the program (that is, correcting the errors in the program) is simply part of the coding process and becomes easier with practice. You may even find that it becomes part of the fun of coding.

KEY TAKEAWAYS

- R is available from the Comprehensive R Archive Network (CRAN) website.
- Although you can work directly in R, it is far easier to work in an integrated development environment (IDE) such as RStudio (available from the RStudio website).
- You can customize RStudio in a variety of ways.
- It is highly useful to organize your work as RStudio projects.
- Packages vastly extend the capabilities of R beyond what Base R can do.

⚠ You can read data in a variety of formats into R, and also enter data using inline code.

⚠ Debugging your programs is simply part of the coding process, and many sources of help are available.

EXERCISES

1. Use RStudio to create a new project, giving it the name of your choice and locating it in the directory of your choice.

2. Within this new project, create a new R script, giving it the name of your choice.

3. An example data file included in the Tidyverse, named *diamonds*, includes the prices and other attributes of almost 54,000 diamonds. Use the *view()* function to view the diamonds data file.

4. Use the *print()* function to print the first 5 lines of the *diamonds* data file.

5. Use the *head()* function to print the first 10 lines of the *diamonds* data file.

6. Use the *slice()* function to print lines 3 through 7 of the *diamonds* data file, and look to see that they are the same ones that the *head()* function printed just above.

7. Use the *tail()* function to print the last 10 lines of the *diamonds* data file.

## CHAPTER 3

Data Wrangling

CHAPTER OBJECTIVES

▽ Understand how to use the *pipe* in Tidyverse.

▽ Learn key data handling operations: selecting variables, selecting cases, recoding variables, and creating new variables.

▽ Know how to change a variable's type.

▽ Know how to work with categorical variables in R.

▽ Understand how R handles missing data and how to assign missing values to variables.

▽ Accomplish data handling tasks using both Tidyverse and Base R approaches.

In this chapter you will learn how to use R to accomplish fundamental data wrangling tasks, using both Tidyverse and Base R approaches. We work with both approaches so that you have greater understanding and flexibility in your ability to work with R, either on your own or with others on your team. We will first look at what is known as the *pipe* in Tidyverse, which is a key element in the flow of Tidyverse operations. Next, we will cover key data handling operations, including selecting variables, selecting cases, recoding variables, and creating new variables. Along the way, we will explore how R handles missing data and how to assign missing values to variables. After that, we look at how to change a variable's type, how to work with categorical variables in R, and how to merge data files. We will conclude the chapter with a brief discussion of *tidy data*.

Example Data

In this chapter we will use the hypothetical data set shown in Table 3.1. The data are the kind that could emerge from a research or evaluation study comparing participants in two different program groups and that would include the following variables:

- ID: A unique identifier for each participant.
- Program: A categorical variable indicating the specific program in which an individual participated.
- Outcome: A measure of the program outcome.
- Satisfaction: A rating of satisfaction with the program (on a scale of 1 to 5).
- Effort_1 to Effort_5: Five different indicators of how much effort a participant put into the program (each indicator on a scale of 1 to 5).

At this point, go ahead and create a data file called *example_data*, either in Excel or within a script using the *c( )* function (see Chapter 2, the "Entering Data via Inline Code" section), using the data presented in Table 3.1.

TABLE 3.1. Hypothetical Data from a Research or Evaluation Study

ID	Program	Outcome	Satisfaction	Effort_1	Effort_2	Effort_3	Effort_4	Effort_5
1	1	19	4	1	3	3	3	1
2	1	21	3	2	2	3	1	2
3	1	20	1	1	2	2	3	2
4	1	20	3	1	2	3	5	2
5	1	24	3	2	3	4	2	4
6	2	26	2	3	2	1	3	3
7	2	26	3	2	4	3	4	3
8	2	25	2	2	2	1	3	3
9	2	25	3	3	1	3	3	1
10	2	30	3	4	1	3	1	9

The Pipe

Tidyverse Approach

A philosophy of the Tidyverse is that operations are verb-oriented and connected by an operator known as the pipe: "% >%." We can use the keyboard to type this operator in our program, or we can use RStudio's keyboard shortcut: *Ctrl+Shift+M*. The pipe is read as ". . . and then . . ."

Thus, for example, the following code creates a data frame named *example_data* by reading the example_data (in Table 3.1) from an Excel file (named *Example_Data*) ". . . and then . . ." calls the *view()* function to open a tab to view the data.

```
# Load packages
library(tidyverse)
library(readxl)
# Read Data from Excel, assign to a Data frame, and view the data
example_data <- read_excel("Example_Data.xlsx") %>%
  view()
```

Go ahead and run this code in RStudio. Remember, we need to be in the R project with the data file (or else use the full pathname for the file, remembering to use the forward slash (" / ") rather than the backslash (" \ " in the pathname). Also remember that we need to load packages each time we start an R session, though we only need to load them once per session. If we try to run a function and receive a message that it was not found, it means we need to use the *library()* function to load the package that has the function we want to run. If calling the *library()* function returns the message that there is no package with the name that we are trying to load, that means that either the package name was misspelled or incorrectly capitalized, or that the package needs to be installed.

Base R Approach

The pipe does not exist in Base R.

Select Variables

In this section we look at how to select variables from among all those in a data frame. For example, our data frame may have many variables, but our analysis calls for working with only a few of them. In this case, we could create a new data frame that includes only the variables we are interested in. As an example, let's create a new data frame that includes only the ID, Program, and Outcome variables from the *example_data* data frame.

Tidyverse Approach

The *select()* function lets you choose variables based on their names. The following code uses a Tidyverse approach to read the example data file. Then use only the ID, Program, and Outcome variables to create a new data file called *outcome_data*; and view the new data frame. The result will look like Figure 3.1.

```
# Create data frame with only ID, Program and Outcome variables
#    using the select() function
outcome_data <- example_data %>%
  select(ID, Program, Outcome) %>%
  view()
```

Base R Approach

If we want to select variables or cases using a Base R approach, the general format is (note the use of square brackets rather than parentheses):

```
new_data <- old_data[rows, columns]
```

	ID	Program	Outcome
1	1	1	19
2	2	1	21
3	3	1	20
4	4	1	20
5	5	1	24
6	6	2	26
7	7	2	26
8	8	2	25
9	9	2	25
10	10	2	30

FIGURE 3.1. Hypothetical data with selected variables.

Thus, we could use the following code to create a new data frame called *outcome_data2* from the example data file that includes only the ID, Program, and Outcome variables, and then the *view()* function to view the new file (see Figure 3.1). Note in the display code that no rows have been specified (before the first comma inside the square brackets), so all rows will be included. Also, the columns have been chosen using their names, their names have been put in quotation marks, and because there are several variables, they have been combined using the *c()* function.

```
# Create data frame with only ID, Program and Outcome variables
#    by specifying rows and columns
outcome_data2 <- example_data[ , c("ID", "Program", "Outcome")]
view(outcome_data2)
```

Alternatively, you can use the *subset()* function. The general format for using this function to select variables is:

```
new_data <- subset(old_data, select = c(columns))
```

Thus, the following code uses the *subset()* function to create a new data frame called *outcome_data3* from the example data file that includes only the ID, Program, and Outcome variables, and then view the new file (see Figure 3.2). Again, note that the columns have been chosen using their names, their names have been put in quotation marks, and because there are several variables, they have been combined using the *c()* function.

```
# Create data frame with only ID, Program and Outcome variables
#    using the subset() function
outcome_data3 <- subset(example_data,
                  select = c("ID", "Program", "Outcome"))
view(outcome_data3)
```

ID	Program	Outcome	Satisfaction	Effort_1	Effort_2	Effort_3	Effort_4	Effort_5
1	1	1	19	4	1	3	3	3	1
2	2	1	21	3	2	2	3	1	2
3	3	1	20	1	1	2	2	3	2
4	4	1	20	3	1	2	3	5	2
5	5	1	24	3	2	3	4	2	4

FIGURE 3.2. Hypothetical data with selected cases.

Select Cases

In this section we look at how to select cases from among all those in a data frame. For example, our data frame may have many cases, but our analysis calls for working with only a subset of them. In this case, we could create a new data frame that includes only the cases we are interested in. As an example, let's read the example data file and use only the cases in Program 1 to create a new data file called *program1_data*.

Tidyverse Approach

The *filter()* function lets us pick cases based on their values. The following code uses a Tidyverse approach to accomplish this task and then view the new data frame. Note the use of the double equals sign ("==") rather than a single equals sign ("=") to mean "equals to." The result will look like Figure 3.2.

```
# Create data frame with only cases in Program 1
#    using the filter() function
program1_data <- example_data %>%
  filter(Program == 1) %>%
  view()
```

Base R Approach

As noted above, if you want to select variables or cases using a Base R approach, the general format is (note the use of the square brackets rather than parentheses):

```
new_data <- old_data[rows, columns]
```

Also note that we refer to variables in a data frame by using both the data frame name and the variable name, separated by a "$" sign. The general format for referring to a variable in this way is:

```
dataframe$variable
```

Thus, we can use the following Base R code to create a new data frame called *program1_data2* that includes only the cases in Program 1 (see Figure 3.2). Again, note the use of the double equals sign ("==") rather than a single equals sign ("=") to mean "equals to."

```
# Create data frame with only cases in Program 1
#    by specifying rows and columns
program1_data2 <- example_data[example_data$Program == "1",  ]
view(program1_data2)
```

Missing Data (Part I)

R considers missing data to be *Not Available*, and thus it indicates missing data as *NA*. R considers impossible values, such as dividing by zero, to be *Not a Number* (indicated by *NaN*). Several functions are available in R to deal with missing data. Of particular importance are the following:

- You can assign a value of a variable to be treated as missing (for example, in the *example_data* data frame, the value of 9 for the variable Effort_5 represents missing data);
- You can use the *is.na()* function to test for whether a variable has missing data; and
- You can use the *na.rm()* function to tell R to remove NA values from a calculation.

We will address the topic of missing data in more detail first in the "Recode Variables" section and then in the "Missing Data Part II" section of this chapter.

Recode Variables

We often want to recode variables as part of an analysis. We can either create a new variable that is a recoded version of an existing variable (recommended), or we can have an existing variable take on recoded values (if you are sure you no longer need the original values of that variable). Also, sometimes we want to create a new variable and assign a specific value to it. The Tidyverse *mutate()* function lets us add new variables or to modify existing ones as a function of existing variables.

Recode a Variable into Itself (for Example, Assigning Values to Represent Missing Data)

We commonly need to assign a particular value of a variable to be considered as missing data. For example, in the *example_data* data frame, the value of 9 represents missing data for the variable *Effort_5*. The value of 9 was chosen since it is clearly out of range for a rating scale that can only take values between 1 and 5 (though other values could be used to represent missing data). Entering a placeholder to represent missing data is good practice, since if nothing is entered for a case with missing data, it can be difficult to know if that case really had missing data or if a data entry error caused data to be omitted.

Tidyverse Approach

The following code provides an example of using the *mutate()* function to recode a variable into itself, along with the *na_if()* function to indicate that a value of a variable should be considered missing data (that is, the value of 9 for the variable Effort_5 is to be considered missing data).

```
example_data <- example_data %>%
  mutate(Effort_5 = na_if(Effort_5, 9))
```

Starting on the right-hand side of the assignment operator ("<-"), we can read this code as read the *example_data* data frame, and then *mutate* the variable *Effort_5*, recoding a value of 9 to be *NA*. The result is saved by assigning the data frame back to itself (using the assignment operator " <- ").

To see how this works, run the following code and examine the results at each step. Remember, if we have not already loaded the *Tidyverse* and *readxl* packages in our current R session, then we will need to load them before running this code. Also, you can use the *view()* function rather than the *print()* function if you prefer to view the data in a tab rather than in the Console.

```
# Read data from Excel, assign to a data frame, and look at the
#    data in the RStudio Console
# Notice that ID Number 10 has the value or "9" for the variable #
#    Effort_5, to represent missing data
example_data <- read_excel("Example_Data.xlsx") %>%
  print()
```

The result is shown below:

```
> # Read Example Data
> example_data <- read_excel("Example_Data.xlsx") %>%
+   print()
# A tibble: 10 x 9
      ID Program Outcome Satisfaction Effort_1 Effort_2 Effort_3 Effort_4 Effort_5
   <dbl>   <dbl>   <dbl>        <dbl>    <dbl>    <dbl>    <dbl>    <dbl>    <dbl>
 1     1       1      19            4        1        3        3        3        1
 2     2       1      21            3        2        2        3        1        2
 3     3       1      20            1        1        2        2        3        2
 4     4       1      20            3        1        2        3        5        2
 5     5       1      24            3        2        3        4        2        4
 6     6       2      26            2        3        2        1        3        3
 7     7       2      26            3        2        4        3        4        3
 8     8       2      25            2        2        2        1        3        3
 9     9       2      25            3        3        1        3        3        1
10    10       2      30            3        4        1        3        1        9
```

Now enter the following code.

```
# For the variable Effort_5, change the value of "9" to be missing
# Display the data frame in the RStudio Console
# Notice that ID Number 10 now has "NA" for Effort_5
example_data %>%
  mutate(Effort_5 = na_if(Effort_5, 9)) %>%
    print()
```

The result is shown as follows:

```
> example_data %>%
+   mutate(Effort_5 = na_if(Effort_5, 9)) %>%
+   print()
# A tibble: 10 x 9
      ID Program Outcome Satisfaction Effort_1 Effort_2 Effort_3 Effort_4 Effort_5
   <dbl>   <dbl>   <dbl>        <dbl>    <dbl>    <dbl>    <dbl>    <dbl>    <dbl>
 1     1       1      19            4        1        3        3        3        1
 2     2       1      21            3        2        2        3        1        2
 3     3       1      20            1        1        2        2        3        2
 4     4       1      20            3        1        2        3        5        2
 5     5       1      24            3        2        3        4        2        4
 6     6       2      26            2        3        2        1        3        3
 7     7       2      26            3        2        4        3        4        3
 8     8       2      25            2        2        2        1        3        3
 9     9       2      25            3        3        1        3        3        1
10    10       2      30            3        4        1        3        1       NA
```

However, this change was not saved in the data frame. In order to save the change, we need to assign the data frame back to itself. Let's enter and run the following code to see how this works.

```
# Display the data frame again in the RStudio Console
# Notice that ID Number 10 shows "9" since the change was not saved
example_data %>%
  print()

# For the variable Effort_5, change the value of "9" to be missing
#    and assign the change to the same data frame
example_data <- example_data %>%
  mutate(Effort_5 = na_if(Effort_5, 9))

# Display the data frame again in the RStudio Console
# Notice that ID Number 10 shows "NA" since the change was saved
example_data %>%
  print()
```

Base R Approach

The general pattern for using the Base R approach to recode a variable into itself is:

```
dataframe$variable[dataframe$variable == value] <- newvalue
```

Thus, we can use the following line of code to recode a value of 9 for the variable *Effort_5* in the *example_data* data frame so that it is considered to be a missing value:

```
example_data$Effort_5[example_data$Effort_5 == 9] <- NA
```

Note that in this line of code we have (1) referred to the variable explicitly using the *dataframe$variable* notation, (2) used square brackets rather than parentheses, (3) used " == " rather than " = " to mean "equal to," and (4) and used the assignment operator " <- " to replace the value of 9, with *NA* within the same data frame.

To see how this works, run this code and follow the comments to examine the results at each step. You can use the *view()* function rather than the *print()* function if you prefer to view the data in a tab rather than in the Console.

```
# Read data from Excel, assign to a data frame, and look at the
#    data in the RStudio Console
```

```
# Notice that ID Number 10 has the value or "9" for the variable
#   Effort_5, representing which represents missing data
example_data <- read_excel("Example_Data.xlsx")
print(example_data)

# For the variable Effort_5, change the value of "9" to be missing
example_data$Effort_5[example_data$Effort_5 == 9] <- NA

# Display the data frame again in the RStudio Console
# Notice that ID Number 10 shows "NA" since the change was saved
print(example_data)
```

Create a New Variable from an Existing Variable

We commonly want to create a new variable that is a function of an existing variable or variables. For instance, our *example_data* data frame has five variables representing different aspects of level of effort. Let's create a new variable, *total_effort*, that is the sum of these five variables.

Tidyverse Approach

The following code provides an example of using the *mutate()* function to create a new variable based on existing variables. This example uses *mutate()* to create the new variable *total_effort*, which is the sum of the five variables representing level of effort.

```
# Compute total_effort as the sum of Effort_1 to Effort_5
example_data <- example_data %>%
  mutate(total_effort = (Effort_1 +
                          Effort_2 +
                          Effort_3 +
                          Effort_4 +
                          Effort_5))
```

Starting on the right-hand side of the assignment operator ("<-"), we can read this as: read the *example_data* data frame, and then use the *mutate* function to create the variable total_effort as the sum of variables *Effort_1*, *Effort_2*, *Effort_3*, *Effort_4*, and *Effort_5*. The result is saved by assigning the data frame back to itself (using the assignment operator "<-").

It is a good idea to check that the computer did what we intended it to do, so let's use the *select(),*and *print()* functions to show in the Console the five original variables and the new variable (we can expect that the computer did what we told it to do, but if there are problems with the code, then what we told it to do and what we intended it to do may not align, and corrections will need to be made). You can glance at this output to confirm that the new variable is indeed the sum of these five variables. Note that for ID = 20 the value for *total_effort* is *NA*; since the value of *Effort_5* for that case was *NA*, the computed new variable is also *NA*. We will look further into handling NA values in a later section of this chapter. Also, note that the data frame was not assigned back to itself (there is no assignment operator "<-"). Thus, in this example, the *select()* function determines what is displayed in the Console but does not modify the data frame.

```
# Check computation of total_effort
example_data %>%
 select(ID, Effort_1, Effort_2, Effort_3, Effort_4, Effort_5,
        total_effort) %>%
 print()
```

The result is as follows:

```
> example_data %>%
+       select(ID, Effort_1, Effort_2, Effort_3, Effort_4, Effort_5,
+                 total_effort) %>%
+       print()
# A tibble: 10 x 7
      ID Effort_1 Effort_2 Effort_3 Effort_4 Effort_5 total_effort
   <dbl>    <dbl>    <dbl>    <dbl>    <dbl>    <dbl>        <dbl>
    1       1        1        3        3        3        1           11
    2       2        2        2        3        1        2           10
    3       3        1        2        2        3        2           10
    4       4        1        2        3        5        2           13
    5       5        2        3        4        2        4           15
    6       6        3        2        1        3        3           12
    7       7        2        4        3        4        3           16
    8       8        2        2        1        3        3           11
    9       9        3        1        3        3        1           11
   10      10        4        1        3        1       NA           NA
```

As mentioned in Chapter 2, we have other functions available to select rows to display in the Console. We can use the *head()* function to display the first rows of a data frame, the *tail()* function to display the last rows of the data frame, and the *slice()* function to print selected rows of the data frame. We can also specify the number of rows for the *print()*, *head()*, and *tail()* functions to print (for example, *head(n = 8)* prints the first 8 rows). We use the *slice()* function in the following code to display rows 1 to 3 and rows 8 to 10, along with the selected variables (note the use of the colon " : " to indicate a range, in this example rows 1 through 3 and rows 8 through 10).

```
# Check computation of total_effort (selected rows and columns)
example_data %>%
  select(ID, Effort_1, Effort_2, Effort_3, Effort_4, Effort_5,
         total_effort) %>%
  slice(1:3, 8:10) %>%
  print()
```

As a second example, we will use the *case_when()* function to create a new variable from an existing variable, recoding values of the existing variable. This function is a general version of the *ifelse()* function (which we could use instead, although the *case_when()* function is easier to use when testing multiple conditions). In this example, we create a new variable named *Program_recoded* that is based on the existing *Program* variable but recodes the value *2* to the value *0*. The following lines accomplish this task and then check the work. Notice that the assignment of values to the new *Program_recoded* variable involves a single equals sign (" = "), and that the test of the values for the existing *Program* variable involves two equals signs (" == "). The tilde (" ~ ") is used to separate the left and right sides of an equation. We can understand the *mutate()* function in the following code as: when the variable *Program* has a value of *1*, assign the value of *1* to the variable *Program_recoded*; and when the variable *Program* has a value of *2*, assign the value of *0* to the variable *Program_recoded*.

```
# Create new variable with Program value of 2 recoded to a value of 0
example_data <- example_data %>%
  mutate(Program_recoded = case_when(
    Program == 1 ~ 1,
    Program == 2 ~ 0))

# List cases to check work
example_data %>%
  select(ID, Program, Program_recoded) %>%
  print()
```

The result is shown below.

```
> # Create new variable with Program value of 2 recoded to a value of 0
> example_data <- example_data %>%
+    mutate(Program_recoded = case_when(
+       Program == 1 ~ 1,
+       Program == 2 ~ 0))
> # List cases to check work
> example_data %>%
+    select(ID, Program, Program_recoded) %>%
+    print()
# A tibble: 10 x 3
      ID Program Program_recoded
   <dbl>   <dbl>           <dbl>
 1     1       1               1
 2     2       1               1
 3     3       1               1
 4     4       1               1
 5     5       1               1
 6     6       2               0
 7     7       2               0
 8     8       2               0
 9     9       2               0
10    10       2               0
```

As a third example, we will use the *case_when()* function to again create a new variable from an existing variable, grouping values of the existing variable into fewer categories. In this example, we create a new variable named *Satisfaction_recoded*, which is based on the existing *Satisfaction* variable but recodes the values of 1 and 2 to the value 1, recodes the value of 3 to the value 2, and recodes the values 4 and 5 to the value 3. The following lines accomplish this task and then check the work. Notice again that the assignment of values to the new *Satisfaction_recoded* variable involves a single equals sign (" = "), and that the test of the values for the existing *Program* variable involves the %in% operator (this operator checks whether a value, such as 1, exists in the named variable, which is *Satisfaction* in this example). Also, notice that the *c()* function is used to indicate the values of the existing variables that will be grouped together. The tilde (" ~ ") is again used to separate the left and right sides of an equation. We can understand the *mutate()* function in the following code as: when the variable *Satisfaction* has a value of 1 or 2, assign the value 1 to the variable *Satisfaction_recoded*; when the variable *Satisfaction* has a value of 3, assign the value of 2 to the variable *Satisfaction_recoded*; and when the variable *Satisfaction* has a value of *4* or *5*, assign the value *3* to the variable *Satisfaction_recoded*.

```
# Create new variable with Satisfaction recoded into fewer values
example_data <- example_data %>%
  mutate(Satisfaction_recoded = case_when(
    Satisfaction %in% c(1, 2) ~ 1,
    Satisfaction %in% c(3) ~ 2,
    Satisfaction %in% c(4, 5) ~ 3))

# List cases to check work
example_data %>%
  select(ID, Satisfaction, Satisfaction_recoded) %>%
  print()
```

The result is shown below.

```
> # Create new variable with Satisfaction recoded into fewer values
> example_data <- example_data %>%
+   mutate(Satisfaction_recoded = case_when(
+     Satisfaction %in% c(1, 2) ~ 1,
+     Satisfaction %in% c(3) ~ 2,
+     Satisfaction %in% c(4, 5) ~ 3))
> # List cases to check work
> example_data %>%
+   select(ID, Satisfaction, Satisfaction_recoded) %>%
+   print()
# A tibble: 10 x 3
      ID Satisfaction Satisfaction_recoded
   <dbl>        <dbl>                <dbl>
 1     1            4                    3
 2     2            3                    2
 3     3            1                    1
 4     4            3                    2
 5     5            3                    2
 6     6            2                    1
 7     7            3                    2
 8     8            2                    1
 9     9            3                    2
10    10            3                    2
```

Base R Approach

The general pattern for using the Base R approach to create a new variable based on existing variables is:

```
dataframe$newvariable <- some function of dataframe$oldvariable(s)
```

Thus, we could use the following code to create a new variable called *total_effort2* whose value is the sum of variables *Effort_1*, *Effort_2*, *Effort_3*, *Effort_4*, and *Effort_5*:

```
# Compute total_effort2 as the sum of Effort_1 to Effort_5
example_data$total_effort2 <- example_data$Effort_1 +
  example_data$Effort_2 +
  example_data$Effort_3 +
  example_data$Effort_4 +
  example_data$Effort_5
```

You can use the next lines of code to display in the Console particular variables to check that the computer did what you intended to do. The result is similar to what we saw above.

```
# Check computation of total_effort2
example_data[ , c("ID", "Effort_1", "Effort_2", "Effort_3",
"Effort_4","Effort_5", "total_effort2")]
```

In looking at this code, recall that we can display in the Console in different ways:

- The contents of a data frame by entering and running just its name,
- Selected rows and all columns of a data frame using the format dataframe[rows,],
- Selected columns and all rows of a data frame using the format dataframe[, cols], and
- Use of the *c()* function in selecting rows or columns to display.

For example, we can use the following code to first display the entire *example_data* data frame, and to then display only rows 1 through 3 and rows 8 through 10 along with columns *ID*, *Effort_1*, *Effort_2*, *Effort_3*, *Effort_4*, *Effort_5*, and *total_effort2* (notice that the columns have been enclosed in parentheses).

```
# Display the entire data frame
example_data
# Check computation of List total_effort2 (selected rows and columns)
example_data[ c(1:3, 8:10), c("ID", "Effort_1", "Effort_2", "Effort_3",
"Effort_4", "Effort_5", "total_effort2")]
```

Create a New Variable and Assign a Specific Value

Sometimes we want to create a new variable and assign a specific value to it. For example, we might be reading and merging data from different sites and we want to keep track of which data came from which site, but the data do not include a variable that indicates which site they came from. Similarly, we might be reading and merging data collected by different researchers, and so we want to keep track of which data was collected by which researcher; however, the data do not include a variable indicating which researcher collected the data.

Tidyverse Approach

The following code uses the *mutate()* function to create two new variables and assign a specific value to each of them. We create a new variable called *Site* and assign it a value of *1*, and we create a new variable called *Researcher* and assign it a value of *Researcher_1*. The code then displays the first five lines of the data frame, showing the ID and two new variables.

```
# Create new variables for "site" and "researcher" and assign values
example_data <- example_data %>%
  mutate(Site = 1) %>%
  mutate(Researcher = "Researcher_1")

example_data %>%
  select("ID", "Site", "Researcher") %>%
  print()
```

Notice that since the value Researcher_1 is a character string, it is enclosed in quotation marks. Also, notice that the because of the assignment operator ("<-") in the first three lines of code, the *mutate()* function creates two variables that are added to the data frame. However, the second three lines of code do not assign the result of running the code to the data frame object, so the *select()* function affects what is displayed in the Console but does not affect the data frame itself.

```
> example_data <- example_data %>%
+     mutate(Site = 1) %>%
+     mutate(Researcher = "Researcher_1")
> example_data %>%
+     select("ID", "Site", "Researcher") %>%
```

```
+    print ()
# A tibble: 10 x 3
        ID  Site Researcher
     <dbl> <dbl> <chr>
 1      1     1 Researcher_1
 2      2     1 Researcher_1
 3      3     1 Researcher_1
 4      4     1 Researcher_1
 5      5     1 Researcher_1
 6      6     1 Researcher_1
 7      7     1 Researcher_1
 8      8     1 Researcher_1
 9      9     1 Researcher_1
10     10     1 Researcher_1
```

Base R Approach

The following code uses a Base R approach to create two new variables and assign a specific value to each of them. We create a new variable called *Site* and assign it a value of *1*, and we create a new variable called *Researcher* and assign it a value of *Researcher_1*. Notice that since the value Researcher_1 is a character string, it is enclosed in quotation marks. The code then displays the data frame, showing the ID and two new variables. The result is the same as shown above.

```
# Create new variables for "site" and "researcher" and assign values
example_data$Site <- 1
example_data$Researcher <- "Researcher_1"
example_data[ , c("ID", "Site", "Researcher")]
```

The following code uses a Base R approach to create the new variable *Program_recoded*, based on values of the variable *Program*, and recodes the value of *2* for the variable *Program* to a value of *0* for the variable *Program_recoded*. The result is the same as shown above.

```
# Create new variable with Program value of 2 recoded to a value of 0
example_data$Program_recoded [example_data$Program == 1] <- 1
example_data$Program_recoded [example_data$Program == 2] <- 0
example_data[ , c("ID", "Program", "Program_recoded")]
```

The following code uses a Base R approach to create the new variable *Satisfaction_recoded*, based on values of the variable *Satisfaction*, recoding the values *1* and *2* for the variable *Satisfaction* to the value of

1 for the variable *Satisfaction_recoded*; recoding the value *3* for the variable *Satisfaction* to the value *1* for the variable *Satisfaction_recoded*; and recoding the values *4* and *5* for the variable *Satisfaction* to the value *3* for the variable *Satisfaction_recoded*. The result is the same as shown above.

```
# Create new variable with Satisfaction recoded into fewer values
example_data$Satisfaction_recoded [example_data$Satisfaction == 1] <- 1
example_data$Satisfaction_recoded [example_data$Satisfaction == 2] <- 1
example_data$Satisfaction_recoded [example_data$Satisfaction == 3] <- 2
example_data$Satisfaction_recoded [example_data$Satisfaction == 4] <- 3
example_data$Satisfaction_recoded [example_data$Satisfaction == 5] <- 3
example_data[ , c("ID", "Satisfaction", "Satisfaction_recoded")]
```

Arithmetic and Logical Operators

R has a wide variety of operators that can be used when operating on existing variables or when creating new variables. Some commonly used arithmetic and logical operators include:

Operator	Operation
–	Subtraction
+	Addition
!	Not
:	Sequence
*	Multiplication
/	Division
^	Exponentiation
<	Less than
>	Greater than
==	Equal to
>=	Greater than or equal to
<=	Less than or equal to
&	And
|	Or

Additional operators and their operations can be found in Section *3.1.4 Operators* at *https://cran.r-project.org/doc/manuals/r-release/R-lang. html.*

Missing Data (Part II)

R has several functions for handling missing data. Now that we have worked with missing data a bit, let's look at two of them

Testing for Missing Data

We can use the *is.na()* function to test whether or not a case has missing data for a particular variable. The general format is:

```
is.na(dataframe$variable)
```

If you run this line of code, you will see output in the Console that shows *TRUE* or *FALSE* for each case, depending on whether the case has missing data (TRUE) or does not have missing data (FALSE) for that variable. As an example, the following code tests for missing data for the variable *Effort_5*:

```
# Test for missing data in variable Effort_5
is.na(example_data$Effort_5)
```

If we run this code, we will see *FALSE* for the first nine cases and *TRUE* for the tenth case, as is expected if we have previously identified the value 9 as missing data for the variable *Effort_5* in this data frame.

```
> is.na(example_data$Effort_5)
 [1] FALSE FALSE FALSE FALSE FALSE FALSE FALSE FALSE FALSE TRUE
```

We can find the particular case(s) with missing data using either a Tidyverse or Base R approach, as shown in the following lines of code. Here we display only the variables ID and Effort_5 (that is, the only variables of interest in this example).

```
# Identify case(s) with missing data for variable Effort_5
#    Tidyverse approach
```

```
example_data %>%
  select (ID, Effort_5) %>%
  filter(is.na(Effort_5)) %>%
  print()

# Identify case(s) with missing data for variable Effort_5
#    Base R approach
example_data[is.na(example_data$Effort_5), c("ID", "Effort_5")]
```

The results look like this:

```
> # Identify case(s) with missing data for variable Effort_5
> #    Tidyverse approach
> example_data %>%
+   select (ID, Effort_5) %>%
+   filter(is.na(Effort_5)) %>%
+   print()
# A tibble: 1 x 2
     ID Effort_5
  <dbl>    <dbl>
1    10       NA
```

Remove Missing Data from a Calculation

If a variable has missing values, it will cause the results of a calculation to also be missing, unless we instruct R not to include the missing values in the calculation. Note that this is also true when running a function that involves calculations, such as a statistical test. We can use the *na.rm()* function to instruct R to remove NA values from a calculation. To illustrate, let's look at the mean for the variable Effort_5:

```
# Compute the mean for Effort_5
mean(example_data$Effort_5)
```

If we run this code, we will see in the Console that the mean for this variable is missing (that is, *NA*), since one of the cases has missing data for this variable. Thus, to calculate the mean for this variable, we need to instruct R to remove the missing data from the calculation:

```
# Compute the mean for Effort_5
mean(example_data$Effort_5, na.rm = TRUE)
```

If we run this code, we will see that the mean, based on the cases with nonmissing data, is 2.333333. Depending on our purpose, we may wish to round the result in the output, for example, to two decimal places, which yields a mean of 2.33:

```
# Compute the mean for Effort_5
round(mean(example_data$Effort_5, na.rm = TRUE), 2)  ·
>    # Compute the mean for Effort_5
>    round(mean(example_data$Effort_5, na.rm = TRUE), 2)
[1] 2.33
```

Identify and Change Variable Types

R has several data types, including: numeric, character, and logical data. Numeric data contain numbers, character data contain letters (and possibly numbers), and logical data contain TRUE or FALSE depending on the logical condition (that is, whether the condition is true or false, for example, when we use the *is.factor()* function on the following pages to test whether or not a variable is a factor). We can use the *str()* function to compactly display the internal structure of an R object. The following code displays in the Console the structure of the *example_data* data frame:

```
# Display the structure of a data frame
str(example_data)
```

In the output, we can see the names of the variables, their data type, and the values of each variable for the first cases. For example (and as expected), *ID* is a numeric variable; the first 10 values are *1* through *10*, and *Researcher* is a character variable that has *Researcher_1* as the value for the first cases.

```
>    # Display the structure of a data frame
>    str(example_data)
tibble [10 x 13] (S3: tbl_df/tbl/data.frame)
 $ ID           : num [1:10] 1 2 3 4 5 6 7 8 9 10
 $ Program      : num [1:10] 1 1 1 1 1 2 2 2 2 2
 $ Outcome      : num [1:10] 19 21 20 20 24 26 26 25 25 30
 $ Satisfaction : num [1:10] 4 3 1 3 3 2 3 2 3 3
 $ Effort_1     : num [1:10] 1 2 1 1 2 3 2 2 3 4
 $ Effort_2     : num [1:10] 3 2 2 2 3 2 4 2 1 1
 $ Effort_3     : num [1:10] 3 3 2 3 4 1 3 1 3 3
 $ Effort_4     : num [1:10] 3 1 3 5 2 3 4 3 3 1
 $ Effort_5     : num [1:10] 1 2 2 2 4 3 3 3 1 NA
```

```
$ total_effort2: num [1:10] 11 10 10 13 15 12 16 11 11 18
$ total_effort : num [1:10] 11 10 10 13 15 12 16 11 11 NA
$ Site         : num [1:10] 1 1 1 1 1 1 1 1 1 1
$ Researcher   : chr [1:10] "Researcher_1" "Researcher_1"
"Researcher_1" "Researcher_1" ...
```

Of particular interest to us here is the *Program* variable. In the *example_data* data frame, *Program* is a numeric variable. However, our intention is that it be a categorical variable that identifies the two different programs, and it just happens to use numbers rather than words to identify the values of the variable (that is, *1* instead of *One,* and *2* instead of *Two*). Thus, the *Program* variable cannot be used in an analysis that requires it to be categorical (for example, an independent samples *t*-test) until it is converted to a categorical variable. In R, categorical variables are called *factors* (R has a variety of functions that can be applied to categorical variables, available through the *Forcats* package).

We can use functions to test whether or not a variable is of a certain type, for example, by using *is.numeric(), is.character(), is.factor(),* or similar functions (similar to the *is.na()* function we saw above). We can also use functions to change a variable's data type, for example, by using *as.numeric(), as.character(), as.factor()* or similar functions. Let's see this in action by using the following code to change *Program* from a numeric variable to a factor and let's check the work along the way:

```
# Check the structure of the Program variable
str(example_data$Program)

# Alternatively, test whether the Program variable is a factor
is.factor(example_data$Program)

# Change the Program variable data type to factor
example_data$Program <- factor(example_data$Program)

# Re-check the structure of the Program variable
str(example_data$Program)

# Alternatively, re-test whether the Program variable is a factor
is.factor(example_data$Program)
```

We can see the results displayed in the Console, confirming that the variable has been changed to a factor with two levels (that is, "1" and "2").

```
>    # Check the structure of the Program variable
>    str(example_data$Program)
 num [1:10] 1 1 1 1 1 2 2 2 2 2
>    # Alternatively, test whether the Program variable is a factor
>    is.factor(example_data$Program)
[1] FALSE
>    # Change the Program variable data type to factor
>    example_data$Program <- factor(example_data$Program)
>    # Re-check the structure of the Program variable
>    str(example_data$Program)
 Factor w/ 2 levels "1","2": 1 1 1 1 1 2 2 2 2 2
>    # Alternatively, re-test whether the Program variable is a factor
>    is.factor(example_data$Program)
[1] TRUE
```

Notice that that in the line Factor w/ 2 levels "1","2": 1 1 1 1 1 2 2 2 2 2 we see that the factor has two levels, that these are labeled "1" and "2," and that the underlying data are still numeric.

Change Factor Value Labels

We can also use the *factor()* function to change the labels associated with the values of the variable. As an example, we will consider the variable *Effort_1*. First, we look at the structure of this variable by running these lines of code (we re-read the data so that it is in its original form):

```
example_data <- read_excel("Example_Data.xlsx")
str(example_data$Effort_1)
```

In the R Console, we see that this is a numeric variable:

```
> str(example_data$Effort_1)
 num [1:10] 1 2 1 1 2 3 2 2 3 4
```

If we convert this variable to a factor, as above, and then look at its structure again, we will see that it has become a factor and that the factor labels are the same as the factor values:

```
example_data$Effort_1 <- factor(example_data$Effort_1)
str(example_data$Effort_1)
```

Running the code above produces this result:

```
> str(example_data$Effort_1)
Factor w/ 4 levels "1","2","3","4": 1 2 1 1 2 3 2 2 3 4
```

However, we can use the *factor()* function to also change the value labels to be more descriptive; for example, this code

```
example_data$Effort_1 <- factor(example_data$Effort_1,
                                levels = c(1, 2, 3, 4, 5),
                                labels = c(            "Very Low",
                                                       "Low",
                                                       "Moderate",
                                                       "High",
                                                       "Very High"))
str(example_data$Effort_1)
```

produces this result:

```
> str(example_data$Effort_1)
Factor w/ 5 levels "Very Low","Low",..: 1 2 1 1 2 3 2 2 3 4
```

These value labels help our output to be more readable. However, it is not as easy to assign labels to variables. Some packages, for example, *Hmisc* and *expss*, have some ability to label variables that may be helpful. Other packages, such as *flextable*, have the ability to change labels produced in output to help make the output (such as tables) more readable.

Join Data Frames

We often want to combine data from two or more data frames into a single data frame. This commonly takes one of three forms. First, we may want to add cases with the same variables from different data frames. For example, a researcher may collect the same data from different groups of people which is entered into different data files, and then we want to combine those data files (that is, the combined file has the same number of variables but more cases; this is sometimes called adding cases or appending files). Second, a researcher may collect different data from the same people, which is entered into different data files, and then we want to combine those files (that is, the combined file has the same number of cases but more variables for each case; this is sometimes called merging files). Third, a researcher may want to combine files that contain data from different units of analysis, where a case in one file contains data that are relevant to more than one case in the other file (for example, if one file contains student-level data and the other file contains school-level data; this is sometimes called a table lookup).

Let's look at these different methods of joining data frames. To begin, create four data frames with the data in the tables below. You can do this either by entering the data into Excel or by entering it using R code (shown below).

Data Frame A

ID	Group	Variable 1	Variable 2
1	A	11	21
2	A	12	22
3	A	13	23
4	A	14	24
5	A	15	25

Data Frame B

ID	Group	Variable 1	Variable 2
6	B	16	26
7	B	17	27
8	B	18	28
9	B	19	29
10	B	20	30

Data Frame C

ID	Variable 3
1	a
2	b
5	e
6	f
9	i
10	j

Data Frame D

Group	Variable 4
A	1
B	2

Here is the R code for creating the four tables above:

```
# Create and view data frame A
ID <- c(1, 2, 3, 4, 5)
group <- c("A", "A", "A", "A", "A")
variable_1 <- c(11, 12, 13, 14, 15)
variable_2 <- c(21, 22, 23, 24, 25)
dataframe_a <- data.frame(ID, group, variable_1, variable_2)
dataframe_a
```

```
# Create and view data frame B
ID <- c(6, 7, 8, 9, 10)
group <- c("B", "B", "B", "B", "B")
variable_1 <- c(16, 17, 18, 19, 20)
variable_2 <- c(26, 27, 28, 29, 30)
dataframe_b <- data.frame(ID, group, variable_1, variable_2)
dataframe_b

# Create and view data frame C—
ID <- c(1, 2, 5, 6, 9, 10)
variable_3 <- c("a", "b", "e", "f", ""","""")
dataframe_c <- data.frame(ID, variable_3)
dataframe_c
+
# Create and view data frame D
group <- c"""","""")
variable_4 <- c(1, 2)
dataframe_d <- data.frame(group, variable_4)
dataframe_d
```

Tidyverse Approach

Let's look at combining these data frames. First, we will combine Data Frame A and Data Frame B. This is done using the *bind_rows()* function. The result is that we have added cases but not variables:

```
# Create and view dataframe_ab by combining Data Frames A and B
dataframe_ab <- bind_rows(dataframe_a, dataframe_b)
dataframe_ab

> # Create and view dataframe_ab by combining Data Frames A and B
> dataframe_ab <- bind_rows(dataframe_a, dataframe_b)
> dataframe_ab
   ID group variable_1 variable_2
1   1    A         11         21
2   2    A         12         22
3   3    A         13         23
4   4    A         14         24
5   5    A         15         25
6   6    B         16         26
7   7    B         17         27
8   8    B         18         28
9   9    B         19         29
10 10    B         20         30
```

Next, we will combine Data Frame AB and Data Frame C using the *left_join()* function. This function keeps all the cases in the table on the left (that is, the one listed first) regardless of whether there is a match in the table on the right.[1] The result is that we have added variables but not cases. Notice that *variable_3* contains *NA* for those cases with missing data.

```
dataframe_abc <- left_join(dataframe_ab, data_frame_c, by = "ID") %>%
   print()
> # Create and view dataframe_abc by combining Data Frames AB and C
> dataframe_abc <- left_join(dataframe_ab, dataframe_c, by = "ID") %>%
+    print()
   ID group variable_1 variable_2 variable_3
1   1     A         11         21          a
2   2     A         12         22          b
3   3     A         13         23       <NA>
4   4     A         14         24       <NA>
5   5     A         15         25          e
6   6     B         16         26          f
7   7     B         17         27       <NA>
8   8     B         18         28       <NA>
9   9     B         19         29          i
10 10     B         20         30          j
```

Finally, we will combine Data Frame ABC and Data Frame D by again using the *left_join()* function. The result is that we have again added variables but not cases, but this time as a table lookup where there is a many-to-one relationship between the tables (that is, a value in one case in Data Frame D relates to many cases in Data Frame ABC.

```
dataframe_abcd <- dataframe_abc %>%
   left_join(dataframe_d, key = "group") %>%
   print()

> # Create and view dataframe_abcd by combining Data Frames ABC and D
> dataframe_abcd <- dataframe_abc %>%
+    left_join(dataframe_d, key = "group") %>%
+    print()
Joining, by = "group"
```

---

[1] The *right_join()* function keeps all the cases in the table on the right regardless of whether there is a match in the table on the left; the *inner_join()* function keeps the cases that have a match in both files; and the *full_join()* function keeps all the cases in both files regardless of whether there is a match in one file or the other.

```
   ID group variable_1 variable_2 variable_3 variable_4
1   1     A         11         21          a          1
2   2     A         12         22          b          1
3   3     A         13         23       <NA>          1
4   4     A         14         24       <NA>          1
5   5     A         15         25          e          1
6   6     B         16         26          f          2
7   7     B         17         27       <NA>          2
8   8     B         18         28       <NA>          2
9   9     B         19         29          i          2
10 10     B         20         30          j          2
```

Base R Approach

The following code uses a Base R approach to accomplish the tasks we completed above. In the *merge()* function, the first dataframe is considered the *x* dataframe, and the second dataframe is considered the *y* data frame. Hence, the option *all.x = TRUE* instructs R to perform a left join and keep all the cases in *dataframe_ab* regardless of whether there is a match in *dataframe_c*.[2]

```
# Create and view dataframe_ab by combining Data Frames A and B
dataframe_ab <- rbind(dataframe_a, dataframe_b)
dataframe_ab

# Create and view dataframe_abc by combining Data Frames AB and C
dataframe_abc <- merge(dataframe_ab, dataframe_c, all.x = TRUE)
dataframe_abc

# Create and view dataframe_abcd by combining Data Frames ABC and D
dataframe_abcd <- merge(dataframe_abc, dataframe_d, all.x = TRUE)
dataframe_abcd
```

Aggregate (Summarize) Data

We sometimes want to aggregate (summarize) data for use in a subsequent analysis. For example, we may want to use the average of the *Outcome* and *total_effort* variables for different groups in the *example_data* data frame. We may also want those values stored in a different data frame. In this section we will look at how to aggregate a data frame.

_____

[2] For a right join in Base R use merge(x, y, all.y = TRUE), for an inner join use merge(x, y), and for a full join use merge(x, y, all.x = TRUE; all.y = TRUE).

Tidyverse Approach

We will use the Tidyverse functions *group_by()* and *summarize()* to aggregate data and save the result to a new data frame. The *group_by()* function allows us to perform any Tidyverse operation "by group" (that is, separately for each group). The *summarize()* function summarizes a variable(s) according to some function. For example, let's use the *example_data* data frame to create a new data frame that for each program group contains the number in the group, the average of the *Outcome* variable, and the average of the *total_effort* variable. We can do that with the following code:

```
# Aggregate (summarize) data into a new data frame
example_data_agg <- example_data %>%
  group_by(Program) %>%
  summarize(n = n(),
            agg_Outcome = mean(Outcome),
            agg_total_effort = mean(total_effort, na.rm = TRUE)) %>%
  print()
```

This code starts with the *example_data* data frame, then it groups by the *Program* variable, and finally it summarizes the data by creating three new variables (one with the number of cases in the group, one with the mean of the *Outcome* variable, and one with the mean of the *total_effort* variable) and displays the result in the Console. The result is saved in the *example_data_agg* data frame.

```
> # Aggregate (summarize) data into a new data frame
> example_data_agg <- example_data %>%
+   group_by(Program) %>%
+   summarize(n = n(),
+             agg_Outcome = mean(Outcome),
+             agg_total_effort = mean(total_effort, na.rm = TRUE)) %>%
+   print()
`summarise()` ungrouping output (override with `.groups` argument)
# A tibble: 2 x 4
  Program     n agg_Outcome agg_total_effort
  <fct>   <int>       <dbl>            <dbl>
1 1           5        20.8             11.8
2 2           5        26.4             12.5
```

Base R Approach

The following code uses a Base R approach to accomplish the tasks we completed above, using the *aggregate()* function. This function includes the name of the data frame being used (that is, *example_data*), the names of the variables to be used for grouping (that is, *by* = *list(example_ data_program)*), and the aggregating function (that is, *FUN* = *mean*), and removes the missing values from the calculation (that is, *na.rm* = *TRUE*). The result is saved in the *example_data_agg* data frame.

```
example_data_agg <- aggregate(
  example_data,
  by = list(example_data$Program),
  FUN = mean,
  na.rm=TRUE)
example_data_agg
```

The above code, however, aggregates all numeric variables in the data frame. If we want to use only some of the variables, we can use the *subset()* function to select them. The code below creates the *example_data_agg* data frame using only the variables *Program*, *Outcome*, and *total_effort*.

```
example_data_agg <- aggregate(
  subset(example_data, select=c(Program, Outcome, total_effort)),
  by = list(example_data$Program),
  FUN = mean, na.rm=TRUE)
example_data_agg
```

Wide and Long Data Formats

Depending on how it is entered, the data we receive may or may not be in a format usable for our purposes. If that is the case, you will need to reformat the data. In this section we will look at some tools for reformatting data. To begin, we create a data frame with the data in the following table, which represents data collected from six people, divided into two groups, at two points in time. You can enter the data in Excel and then read them into R, or you can enter them in an R script using the code below the table.

ID	Group	Time 1	Time 2
1	A	101	201
2	A	102	202
3	A	103	203
4	B	104	204
5	B	105	205
6	B	106	206

```
# Create variables for dataframe_e
ID <- c(1, 2, 3, 4, 5, 6)
group <- c("A", "A", "A", "B", "B", "B")
time_1 <- c(101, 102, 103, 104, 105, 106)
time_2 <- c(201, 202, 203, 204, 205, 206)

# Create and view dataframe_e
dataframe_e <- data.frame(ID, group, time_1, time_2)
dataframe_e
```

These data are in a *wide format*, since there is one row for each case, with variables distributed across the columns. However, in this table we can consider *Time* as a single variable that has two values (that is, 1 and 2), and we can structure the data in *long format* as shown in the next table (which is necessary for some analytic procedures as well as some R packages such as the *ggplot* graphing package that we will work with later in this book).

ID	Group	Time	Score
1	A	1	101
2	A	1	102
3	A	1	103
4	B	1	104
5	B	1	105
6	B	1	106
1	A	2	201
2	A	2	202

(continued)

ID	Group	Time	Score
3	A	2	203
4	B	2	204
5	B	2	205
6	B	2	206

From the Tidyverse perspective, data are considered *tidy* if (1) each variable has its own column, (2) each observation has its own row, and (3) each value has its own cell. Thus, the table above in long format would be considered tidy, but the table just above that one which is in a wide format would not. This very important concept is worth pondering carefully, so that you are able to apply the concept when necessary.

Restructuring Data from Wide Format to Long Format

In this section we will restructure the data from wide format to long format.

Tidyverse Approach

We use the *pivot_longer()*function to restructure our datafile from wide format to long format and save it as a new data frame.[3] The following code accomplishes this task:

```
dataframe_e_long <- dataframe_e %>%
  pivot_longer(c(time_1, time_2),
               names_to = "Time",
               values_to = "Score")
dataframe_e_long
```

This code creates *dataframe_e_long* by reading *dataframe_e*, and then it gathers the data for the variables *time_1* and *time_2* into a single

---

[3] The *pivot_longer()* function is newer than the *gather()* function, which you may also encounter. The R documentation informs us that: Development on gather() is complete, and for new code we recommend switching to pivot_longer(), which is easier to use, more featureful, and still under active development. df % >% gather("key", "value", x, y, z) is equivalent to df % >% pivot_longer(c(x, y, z), names_to = "key", values_to = "value"). (https://tidyr.tidyverse.org/reference/gather.html)

variable called *Time* while also storing the values for the data collected at the two points of time into a new variable called *Score*. Then it displays the result in the Console.

```
> dataframe_e_long <- dataframe_e %>%
+    pivot_longer(c(time_1, time_2),
+                      names_to = "Time",
+                      values_to = "Score")
> dataframe_e_long
# A tibble: 12 x 4
       ID group Time    Score
   <dbl> <chr> <chr>   <dbl>
 1     1 A     time_1    101
 2     1 A     time_2    201
 3     2 A     time_1    102
 4     2 A     time_2    202
 5     3 A     time_1    103
 6     3 A     time_2    203
 7     4 B     time_1    104
 8     4 B     time_2    204
 9     5 B     time_1    105
10     5 B     time_2    205
11     6 B     time_1    106
12     6 B     time_2    206
```

Base R Approach

We can use the *melt()* function from the *reshape2* package to reformat data in a wide format to data in a long format. The following code accomplishes this task for our data frame. Remember to install and load the package if you have not already done so. The resulting data frame matches what was shown above.

```
# Create and view melted data frame
data_frame_e_melted <- melt(dataframe_e,
                          id = c("ID", "group"),
                          measured = c("time_1", "time_2"))
data_frame_e_melted
```

Restructuring Data from Long Format to Wide Format

In this section we will restructure the data from long format to wide format.

Tidyverse Approach

We use the *pivot_wider()* function to restructure our datafile from long format to wide format, and we save it as a new data frame.[4] For ease of illustration, we will take the data frame we created in the previous section when we went from wide format to long format and change it back into a data frame with a wide format. The following code accomplishes this task:

```
dataframe_e_wide <-  dataframe_e_long %>%
  pivot_wider(names_from = Time,
              values_from = Score)
dataframe_e_wide
```

This code creates *dataframe_e_wide* by reading *dataframe_e_long*, and then it spreads the data for the variable *Time* into two variables called *time_1* and *time_2*, while also storing the values for the data collected at the two points of time into their respective new variables. It then displays the result in the Console. The result matches what is shown above.

Base R Approach

We can use the *dcast()* function from the *reshape2* package to reformat data in long format to data in wide format. The following code accomplishes this task for our data frame. The resulting data frame matches what was shown above.

```
# Create and view cast data frame
data_frame_e_cast <- dcast(data_frame_e_melted,
                           ID + group ~
                           variable,
                           value = value)
data_frame_e_cast
```

---

[4]The *pivot_wider()* function is newer than the *spread()* function, which you may also encounter. The R documentation informs us that: Development on spread() is complete, and for new code we recommend switching to pivot_wider(), which is easier to use, more featureful, and still under active development. df % >% spread(key, value) is equivalent to df % >% pivot_wider(names_from = key, values_from = value). (https://tidyr.tidyverse.org/reference/spread.html)

KEY TAKEAWAYS

- You can use R to take care of a wide variety of data wrangling tasks.

- It is important to become familiar working from both Tidyverse and Base R approaches.

- It is important to understand and be able to work with data in both wide and long formats, and to be able to change a data frame from one format to the other.

- From the Tidyverse perspective, data are considered tidy if (1) each variable has its own column, (2) each observation has its own row, and (3) each value has its own cell.

EXERCISES

1. An example data file included in the Tidyverse, named *diamonds*, includes the prices and other attributes of almost 54,000 diamonds. Use this data file to create a new data file, named *diamonds2*, that includes only the variables *carat, cut, color, clarity*, and *price.*

2. Using the diamonds2 data frame, create a data frame named diamonds3 that contains the first 10 records from diamonds2.

3. Using the diamonds2 data frame, create a data frame named diamonds4 that contains the last 10 records from diamonds2.

4. Combine the diamonds3 and diamonds4 data frames into a new data frame named diamonds5.

5. Using the *diamonds* data frame, use the *group_by()* and *summarize()* functions to show the average price by color.

## CHAPTER 4

Descriptive Statistics, *t*-Tests, One-Way ANOVA, and Chi-Square Test

▽ CHAPTER OBJECTIVES

▽ Become familiar with using R to conduct analyses from both Tidyverse and Base R approaches.

▽ Conduct these analyses: descriptive

statistics, *t*-tests, one-way ANOVA, crosstabulation, and chi-square test.

▽ Continue developing facility using R and RStudio through practice by carrying out the analyses in this chapter.

In this chapter we begin using R to analyze data. Our goal is to become acquainted with the fundamental use of R for analysis tasks, recognizing that we can then build our knowledge of R to use additional features available within any particular function, or to accomplish more complex analysis tasks as needed. In this chapter we use R to generate descriptive statistics, conduct *t*-tests and one-way analysis of variance (ANOVA), examine correlation, and analyze crosstabulated data. As you work through this chapter and, later, as you conduct your own analytic work, you may wish to consider the American Statistical Association's guidance regarding *p*-values and significance testing (Wasserstein and Lazar, 2016; Wasserstein Schirm, and Lazar, 2019).

Descriptive Statistics

In this section we use R to produce frequency distributions and to calculate measures of central tendency.

Frequency Distributions

Tidyverse Approach

Let's look at a frequency distribution for the variable *Satisfaction* in the *example_data* data frame. We can do this by using the *group_by()*, *summarize()*, and *mutate()* functions. The following code accomplishes this task:

```
# Load libraries if not already loaded
library(tidyverse)
library(readxl)
# Create frequency distribution for the variable Satisfaction
example_data %>%
  group_by(Satisfaction) %>%
  summarize(N = n()) %>%
  mutate(Percent = prop.table(N) * 100)
```

We can read these lines of code as: take the *example_data* data frame, and then group by levels of the variable *Satisfaction* (that is, we are going to want counts and percentages for each level); then create the variable *N*, which summarizes the count within each level of *Satisfaction*, and create the variable *Percent*, which shows a proportion table (a table that contains the value of each cell divided by the sum of the cells) for the variable *N* that has been multiplied by 100 to obtain a percentage. The result of running this code is:

```
> # Create frequency distribution for the variable Satisfaction
> example_data %>%
+    group_by(Satisfaction) %>%
+    summarize(N = n()) %>%
+    mutate(Percent = prop.table(N) * 100)
`summarize()` ungrouping output (override with `.groups` argument)
# A tibble: 4 x 3
  Satisfaction     N Percent
         <dbl> <int>   <dbl>
1            1     1      10
2            2     2      20
3            3     6      60
4            4     1      10
```

Note that if this data file was such that the percentages were not so evenly divisible and we therefore wanted to round them to some number of digits, we could do so by changing the last line in the code to read as follows (here we indicate that we want rounding to one digit to occur):

```
mutate(Percent = round((prop.table(N) * 100), digits = 1))
```

As we can see from this output, nearly two-thirds (60%) of those answering this question rated their level of satisfaction as "3," and another 10% rated their level of satisfaction as "4."

Base R Approach

We can also accomplish this task from a Base R approach. We use the *table()* function to see one way this can be done. We will start with a simple line of code and then add to it until we have the output that we want.

First, run the following line of code and notice that it returns two rows in the Console. The first row has the values of the *Satisfaction* variable. The second row has the frequency for each of those values.

```
table(example_data$Satisfaction)
```

Next, we use the *transform()* function to flip the rows and columns in the output. When you run this line of code, you will see an unlabeled column or row of numbers, a column labeled Var1 (that is, the variable *Satisfaction*) with the values for the *Satisfaction* variable, and a column labeled *Freq* that has the frequency of each value of the *Satisfaction* variable.

```
transform(table(example_data$Satisfaction))
```

We can use the column labeled *Freq* for additional operations. This is a very important aspect of R: R output contains objects that you can use again for other purposes. The following lines of code apply the *prop.table()* function to the object *Freq* to create percentages rounded to one digit:

```
transform(table(example_data$Satisfaction),
        Percent = round(prop.table(Freq)*100, digits = 1))
```

Descriptive Statistics

In this section we look at some different ways to use R to obtain descriptive statistics. There are many ways to do so, so pick the one that provides the information you need and is convenient for use in your R script. In this section, we look at some example methods.

Tidyverse Approach

We can use the *get_summary_stats()* function from the *rstatix* package to perform basic statistical analyses (remember to assign the value of *q* to be missing data for the vairable *Effort_5*). The following code provides summary statistics:

```
library(rstatix)
example_data %>%
  get_summary_stats(Effort_1 : Effort_5, Outcome, Satisfaction)
```

The results are shown below. These results include, for each variable chosen, the number of cases, minimum, maximum, median, first, and third quartiles, interquartile range, median absolute deviation, mean, standard deviation, standard error of the mean, and 95% confidence interval of the mean. We did not include the variables *ID* and *Program*, since they are categorical (nominal) variables and are not meaningful for this analysis. As an example, we can see from the output that the minimum Outcome score was 19, the maximum score was 30, and the mean score was 23.6, with a standard deviation of 3.5.

```
> example_data %>%
+   get_summary_stats(Effort_1 : Effort_5, Outcome, Satisfaction)
# A tibble: 7 x 13
    variable        n   min   max median    q1    q3   iqr   mad  mean    sd    se    ci
    <chr>        <dbl> <dbl> <dbl>  <dbl> <dbl> <dbl> <dbl> <dbl> <dbl> <dbl> <dbl> <dbl>
1 Effort_1        10     1     4      2   1.25  2.75   1.5  1.48   2.1  0.994 0.314 0.711
2 Effort_2        10     1     4      2   2     2.75  0.75 0.741   2.2  0.919 0.291 0.657
3 Effort_3        10     1     4      3   2.25  3     0.75 0       2.6  0.966 0.306 0.691
4 Effort_4        10     1     5      3   2.25  3     0.75 0.741   2.8  1.23  0.389 0.879
5 Effort_5        10     1     4      2   2     3     1    1.48   2.33 1     0.333 0.769
6 Outcome         10    19    30   24.5  20.2  25.8   5.5  3.71  23.6  3.50  1.11  2.50
7 Satisfaction    10     1     4      3   2.25  3     0.75 0       2.7  0.823 0.26  0.589
```

R functions generally have a variety of options that you can use to control what the function does. For example, we can choose what results the *get_summary_stats()* function displays in the output by using the *show* option:

```
get_summary_stats(Outcome, show = c("n", "min", "max", "median",
"mean", "sd", "se", "ci"))
```

In addition, we could display these results by a grouping variable using the *group_by()* function. For example, the following code produces summary statistics for each of the two Program groups.

```
example_data %>%
  group_by(Program) %>%
  get_summary_stats(Outcome,
                    show = c("n", "min", "max", "median", "mean",
                             "sd", "se", "ci"))
```

This code produces the selected output shown below.

```
> example_data %>%
+    group_by(Program) %>%
+    get_summary_stats(Outcome,
+                      show = c("n", "min", "max", "median", "mean",
+                               "sd", "se", "ci"))
# A tibble: 2 x 10
  Program variable      n    min    max median   mean     sd     se     ci
    <dbl> <chr>     <dbl> <dbl> <dbl>  <dbl>  <dbl>  <dbl>  <dbl>  <dbl>
1       1 Outcome       5    19     24     20   20.8   1.92   0.86   2.39
2       2 Outcome       5    25     30     26   26.4   2.07  0.927   2.58
```

Another way to obtain descriptive statistics is by using the *skim()* function from the *skimr* package. Note that this function produces some similar and some different output than does the *get_summary_stats()* function, and also that it produces a histogram for each variable. The output also includes different information for different types of variables. Here, we have one kind of information about the factor (that is, categorical) variables and another kind for the numeric variables, as is appropriate. If we only want output for selected variables, we can name them (separated by commas) inside the parentheses of the *skim()* function. The following code loads the *skimr* package and runs the *skimr()* function.

```
library(skimr)
example_data %>%
  skim()
```

This code produces the following output.

```
+    skim()
-- Data Summary ------------------------
```

```
                          Values
Name                      Piped data
Number of rows            10
Number of columns         9

Column type frequency:
  numeric                 9

Group variables           None

-- Variable type: numeric ----------------------------------------------
------------------------------------------
# A tibble: 9 x 11
  skim_variable n_missing complete_rate  mean    sd    p0   p25   p50   p75  p100 hist
* <chr>             <int>         <dbl> <dbl> <dbl> <dbl> <dbl> <dbl> <dbl> <dbl> <chr>
1 ID                    0             1   5.5 3.03      1  3.25   5.5  7.75    10 ▇▇▇▇▇
2 Program               0             1   1.5 0.527     1  1       1.5  2       2 ▇▁▁▁▇
3 Outcome               0             1  23.6 3.50     19 20.2   24.5 25.8    30 ▆▂▂▇▂
4 Satisfaction          0             1   2.7 0.823     1  2.25   3    3       4 ▁▂▁▇▂
5 Effort_1              0             1   2.1 0.994     1  1.25   2    2.75     4 ▃▇▁▅▂
6 Effort_2              0             1   2.2 0.919     1  2      2    2.75     4 ▂▁▇▂▂
7 Effort_3              0             1   2.6 0.966     1  2.25   3    3        4 ▂▁▁▇▂
8 Effort_4              0             1   2.8 1.23      1  2.25   3    3        5 ▂▂▁▇▂
9 Effort_5              1           0.9  2.33 1         1  2      2    3        4 ▂▇▁▇▂
```

Base R Approach

Many Base R functions provide common descriptive statistics. One that produces some simple statistics is the *summary()* function. A larger set of descriptive statistics is produced by the *describe()* function from the *psych* package. Note that in the output the variables *ID* and *Program* have an asterisk next to them which indicates that they are categorical variables. In our example the displayed results for these two variables are not meaningful except for the number of cases. The following code loads the *psych* package and runs the *describe()* function.

```
library(psych)
describe(example_data)
```

This code produces the following output. As we can see in this output, the results are the same as those we saw in the output above.

```
> describe(example_data)
             vars  n  mean   sd median trimmed  mad min max range  skew kurtosis   se
ID              1 10  5.5  3.03   5.5    5.50 3.71   1  10     9  0.00    -1.56 0.96
Program         2 10  1.5  0.53   1.5    1.50 0.74   1   2     1  0.00    -2.19 0.17
Outcome         3 10 23.6  3.50  24.5   23.38 3.71  19  30    11  0.20    -1.28 1.11
Satisfaction    4 10  2.7  0.82   3.0    2.75 0.00   1   4     3 -0.58    -0.45 0.26
Effort_1        5 10  2.1  0.99   2.0    2.00 1.48   1   4     3  0.44    -1.08 0.31
Effort_2        6 10  2.2  0.92   2.0    2.12 0.74   1   4     3  0.43    -0.83 0.29
```

Effort_3	7	10	2.6	0.97	3.0	2.62	0.00	1	4	3	-0.59	-1.02	0.31
Effort_4	8	10	2.8	1.23	3.0	2.75	0.74	1	5	4	0.01	-0.95	0.39
Effort_5	9	9	2.3	1.00	2.0	2.33	1.48	1	4	3	0.07	-1.37	0.33

If we want to describe a single variable, we can use the following code (recall that the Base R notation for specifying a variable is *dataframe$variable*):

```
describe(example_data$Outcome)
```

We can also use the *describeBy()* function to show results by group. For example, the following code produces the results for the variable Outcome (the first variable listed), by Program group (the second variable listed).

```
describeBy(example_data$Outcome, example_data$Program)
```

As we compare the output from these different functions, we notice that there are similarities and differences in which summary statistics are produced. Thus, the choice of which function to use (and therefore which package needs to be installed and loaded) is partly a choice of preference but mainly a matter of which function (or functions) will provide you with the information that you need.

t-Tests

In this section we will look at how to conduct *t*-tests using R.

One-Sample *t*-Test

Let's start by using R to conduct a one-sample *t*-test. We will conduct two tests, one illustrating a nondirectional hypothesis and one illustrating a directional hypothesis. In the first example, the hypothesis is that persons living in an urban environment have anxiety levels that are different from the national average. A measure of anxiety yields a score ranging from 0 (no anxiety) to 80 (high anxiety). The data are shown in Table 4.1. We will test the average score from this group against a national average of 30.

TABLE 4.1.	Anxiety Scores			
34	32	28	32	35
32	28	30	39	32
29	33	34	32	30

Note. From Terrell (2021, p. 158).

Tidyverse Approach

We can enter these data in Excel or use the following lines of code to create the dataframe with a variable named *anxiety_score*. Even though we have only one variable, it can still be a data frame (that is, it is a data frame containing a single variable), which is what the Tidyverse *t_test()* function needs.

```
anxiety_score <- c(34, 32, 28, 32, 35,
              32, 28, 30, 39, 32,
              29, 33, 34, 32, 30)
anxiety_score <- as.data.frame(anxiety_score)
```

Next, we use the following code to obtain the descriptive statistics:

```
get_summary_stats(anxiety_score,
              show = c("n", "min", "max", "median", "mean",
                   "sd", "se", "ci"))
```

This code produces the following results, which are shown in the Console:

```
> get_summary_stats(anxiety_score,
+              show = c("n", "min", "max", "median", "mean", "sd", "se", "ci"))
# A tibble: 1 x 9
  variable          n   min   max median  mean    sd    se    ci
  <chr>         <dbl> <dbl> <dbl>  <dbl> <dbl> <dbl> <dbl> <dbl>
1 anxiety_score    15    28    39     32    32  2.88 0.743  1.59
```

Now we conduct our one-sample *t*-test, using the following code. This code starts with the data frame and then calls the *t_test()* function, names the variable we want to test and uses the formula "~ 1" to indicate that there is only one group, and provides the number that we wish to compare to (that is, "mu = 30" for the national average anxiety score of 30).

```
anxiety_score %>%
  t_test(anxiety_score ~ 1, mu = 30)
```

This code produces the following results, which are shown in the Console. The output names the variable being tested (anxiety score) and the groups (since there is only one group, the second one is *NULL*), and shows us the *t* value (labeled *statistic*), the degrees of freedom, and the probability associated with the test statistic. From this output and the one just above, we see that the mean anxiety score is 32 and the value of the *t*-test statistic is 2.69 on 14 degrees of freedom, with *p* = .018.

```
> anxiety_score %>%
+    t_test(anxiety_score ~ 1, mu = 30)
# A tibble: 1 x 7
   .y.            group1 group2        n statistic    df      p
 * <chr>          <chr>  <chr>     <int>     <dbl> <dbl>  <dbl>
 1 anxiety_score  1      null model   15      2.69    14 0.0176
```

For our next example, we look at the question of whether or not scores on a certification exam from students at a university are higher than the national average. Because we are interested in whether the scores are higher rather than just different, we have a directional hypothesis and use a one-tailed test. The data are shown in Table 4.2.

We can enter these data in Excel or use the following lines of code to create the dataframe with a variable named *exam_score*. As in the previous example, even though we have only one variable, it can still be a data frame (that is, it is a data frame containing a single variable), which is what the Tidyverse *t_test()* function needs.

```
exam_score <- c(810, 800, 810, 810, 810,
                810, 815, 815, 815, 815,
```

TABLE 4.2. Certification Exam Scores

810	800	810	810	810
810	815	815	815	815
810	815	820	830	830
840	835	840	835	850
848	840	844	811	865

Note. From Terrell (2021, p. 166).

```
                    810, 815, 820, 830, 830,
                    840, 835, 840, 835, 850,
                    848, 842, 844, 811, 865)
exam_score <- as.data.frame(exam_score)
```

Next, we use the following code to obtain the descriptive statistics and conduct the *t*-test. Once again this code starts with the data frame, and then it calls the *t_test()* function, names the variable we want to test, uses the formula "~ 1" to indicate that there is only one group, and provides the number that we wish for comparison (that is, "mu = 800" for the national average anxiety score of 800). In addition, we include the alternative = "greater" option since we are performing a one-tailed test of whether our sample mean is greater than the comparison number (that is, 800).

```
get_summary_stats(exam_score,
                  show = c("n", "min", "max", "median", "mean",
                        "sd", "se", "ci"))
exam_score %>%
  t_test(exam_score ~ 1, mu = 800, alternative = "greater")
```

This code produces the following results, which are shown in the Console. In the *t*-test output, we again see the named variable being tested (exam score), the groups (since there is only one group, the second one is *NULL*), the *t* value (labeled *statistic*), the degrees of freedom, and the probability associated with the test statistic. From this output above, we note that the mean exam score is 825 and that the value of the *t*-test statistic is 7.43 on 24 degrees of freedom, with $p < .001$.

```
> get_summary_stats(exam_score,
+                   show = c("n", "min", "max", "median", "mean", "sd", "se", "ci"))
# A tibble: 1 x 9
  variable      n   min   max median  mean    sd    se    ci
  <chr>     <dbl> <dbl> <dbl>  <dbl> <dbl> <dbl> <dbl> <dbl>
1 exam_score   25   800   865    815   825  16.8  3.37  6.95


> exam_score %>%
+   t_test(exam_score ~ 1, mu = 800, alternative = "greater")
# A tibble: 1 x 7
  .y.        group1 group2        n statistic    df            p
* <chr>      <chr>  <chr>     <int>     <dbl> <dbl>        <dbl>
1 exam_score 1      null model   25      7.43    24 0.0000000574
```

Base R Approach

We can conduct one sample *t*-test for our two examples using a Base R approach by running the following code. The results are the same as those shown above, although the formatting is different.

```
t.test(anxiety_score, mu = 30)
t.test(exam_score, mu = 800, alternative = "greater")
```

Independent Samples

Now we will use R to conduct a *t*-test for independent samples. The data are from an example in which high school instructors compare whether the frequency of report cards has an effect on students' intrinsic motivation (half the students receive a report card every week and half receive a report card on their normal nine-week schedule). The resulting data are shown in Table 4.3.

We can enter these data in Excel or use the following lines of code to create the dataframe (I have named the data frame *report_card* and have named the variables *timing* and *motivation*):

```
timing <- c("Weekly", "Weekly", "Weekly", "Weekly", "Weekly",
        "Weekly", "Weekly", "Weekly", "Weekly", "Weekly",
        "Nine-week", "Nine-week", "Nine-week", "Nine-week",
        "Nine-week", "Nine-week", "Nine-week", "Nine-week",
        "Nine-week", "Nine-week")
motivation <- c(75, 68, 87, 80, 65, 80, 82, 75 ,75 ,55,
            69, 68, 69, 72, 69, 68, 64, 68, 67, 68)
timing <- factor(timing)
report_card <- data.frame(timing, motivation)
```

TABLE 4.3. **Report Card Data**

Weekly report cards		9-week report cards	
75	80	69	68
68	82	68	64
87	75	69	68
80	75	72	67
65	55	69	68

Note. From Terrell (2021, p. 204).

Tidyverse Approach

To analyze these data, we will obtain descriptive statistics and conduct Levene's test of homogeneity of variances as well as a *t*-test for independent samples. To do so, we will use the *get_summary_stats()*, *levene_test()*, and *t_test()* functions from the *rstatix* package. The following code accomplishes these tasks:

```
# Get summary statistics
report_card %>%
  group_by(timing) %>%
  get_summary_stats(motivation)

# Conduct Levene's test for homogeneity of variances
report_card %>%
  levene_test(motivation ~ timing, center = mean)

# Conduct t-test for independent samples (equal variances not assumed)
report_card %>%
  t_test(motivation ~ timing, detailed = TRUE)

# Conduct t-test for independent samples (equal variances assumed)
report_card %>%
  t_test(motivation ~ timing, var.equal = TRUE, detailed = TRUE)
```

Notice the use of the tilde (" ~ ") to indicate a formula for Levene's test and the *t*-test, with the format *(dependent variable ~ independent variable)*. Also notice that we have made choices about options for functions, for example, by using the mean to compute the center of each group for Levene's test and by telling the *t_test()* function to print detailed results. Finally, notice that we have conducted the *t*-test twice, once not assuming equal variances (the default for the *t_test()* function) and once assuming equal variances. Of course, if we ran Levene's test and examined the output before running the *t*-test, we could decide at that point whether or not we could assume equal variances and then run the *t*-test only once. In this example, $p = .008$ for Levene's test, so we do not assume equal variances. The mean motivation score for the weekly group is 74.2, and the mean motivation score for the nine-week group is 68.2. The value of the *t*-test statistic is 1.99 on 9.81 degrees of freedom, with $p = .076$. The results are as follows.

```
> # Get summary statistics
> report_card %>%
+   group_by(timing) %>%
```

```
+   get_summary_stats(motivation)
# A tibble: 2 x 14
  timing    variable       n   min   max median    q1    q3   iqr   mad  mean    sd    se    ci
  <fct>     <chr>      <dbl> <dbl> <dbl>  <dbl> <dbl> <dbl> <dbl> <dbl> <dbl> <dbl> <dbl> <dbl>
1 Weekly    motivation    10    55    87     75  69.8    80  10.2  8.90  74.2  9.34  2.95  6.68
2 Nine-week motivation    10    64    72     68  68      69   1    1.48  68.2  1.99 0.629  1.42

> # Conduct Levene's test for homogeneity of variances
> report_card %>%
+   levene_test(motivation ~ timing, center = mean)
# A tibble: 1 x 4
    df1   df2 statistic       p
  <int> <int>     <dbl>   <dbl>
1     1    18      8.88 0.00803

> # Conduct t-test for independent samples (equal variances not assumed)
> report_card %>%
+   t_test(motivation ~ timing, detailed = TRUE)
# A tibble: 1 x 15
  estimate estimate1 estimate2 .y.   group1 group2    n1    n2 statistic      p    df conf.low conf.high method
*    <dbl>     <dbl>     <dbl> <chr> <chr>  <chr>  <int> <int>     <dbl>  <dbl> <dbl>    <dbl>     <dbl> <chr>
1        6      74.2      68.2 moti~ Weekly Nine-~    10    10      1.99 0.0756  9.81   -0.748      12.7 T-test
# ... with 1 more variable: alternative <chr>

> # Conduct t-test for independent samples (equal variances assumed)
> report_card %>%
+   t_test(motivation ~ timing, var.equal = TRUE, detailed = TRUE)
# A tibble: 1 x 15
  estimate estimate1 estimate2 .y.   group1 group2    n1    n2 statistic      p    df conf.low conf.high method
*    <dbl>     <dbl>     <dbl> <chr> <chr>  <chr>  <int> <int>     <dbl>  <dbl> <dbl>    <dbl>     <dbl> <chr>
1        6      74.2      68.2 moti~ Weekly Nine-~    10    10      1.99 0.0624    18   -0.346      12.3 T-test
# ... with 1 more variable: alternative <chr>
```

Base R Approach

We can conduct our independent sample *t*-test using a Base R approach by running the following code. The results are the same as those shown above, although the formatting is different.

```
# Get summary statistics
describeBy(report_card$motivation ~ report_card$timing)


# Conduct Levene's test for homogeneity of variances
leveneTest(report_card$motivation, report_card$timing, center = mean)


# Conduct t-test for independent samples (equal variances not assumed)
t.test(report_card$motivation ~ report_card$timing)


# Conduct t-test for independent samples (equal variances assumed)
t.test(report_card$motivation ~ report_card$timing, var.equal = TRUE)
```

Dependent Samples

We will now use R to conduct a *t*-test for dependent samples. The data represent systolic blood pressure values before and after taking a drug

TABLE 4.4.	Systolic Blood Pressure	
Patient	**Prior**	**After**
1	120	135
2	117	118
3	119	131
4	130	128
5	121	121
6	105	115
7	128	124
8	114	111
9	109	117
10	120	120

Note. Adapted from Terrell (2021, p. 227).

designed to stop migraine headaches for two weeks (the researchers are concerned that the medication may affect blood pressure). These data are shown in Table 4.4.

We can enter these data in Excel or use the following lines of code to create the dataframe (I have named the data frame *bp_study,* and I have labeled the variables *patient, time,* and *bp*):

```
patient <- c(1, 2, 3, 4, 5, 6, 7, 8, 9, 10)
time <- c("Before", "Before", "Before", "Before", "Before", "Before",
        "Before", "Before", "Before", "Before",
        "After", "After","After","After","After", "After",
        "After","After","After","After")
bp <- c(120, 117, 119, 130, 121, 105, 128, 114, 109, 120,
        135, 118, 131, 128, 121, 115, 124, 111, 117, 120)
time <- factor(time)
bp_study <- data.frame(patient, time, bp)
```

Tidyverse Approach

To analyze these data, we will obtain descriptive statistics and conduct a *t*-test for dependent samples. We will use the *get_summary_stats(),* and *t_test()* functions from the *rstatix* package. The following code accomplishes these tasks:

```
# Get summary statistics
bp_study %>%
    group_by(time) %>%
    get_summary_stats(bp)

# Conduct t-test for paired samples
bp_study %>%
    t_test(bp ~ time, paired = TRUE, detailed = TRUE)
```

Note the use of the *paired = TRUE* option for the *t_test()* function to indicate that we are conducting a paired samples *t*-test. The results are shown below.

```
> # Get summary statistics
> bp_study %>%
+    group_by(time) %>%
+    get_summary_stats(bp)

# A tibble: 2 x 14
  time    variable     n   min   max median    q1    q3   iqr   mad  mean    sd    se    ci
  <fct>   <chr>     <dbl> <dbl> <dbl>  <dbl> <dbl> <dbl> <dbl> <dbl> <dbl> <dbl> <dbl> <dbl>
1 Before  bp           10   105   130   120.  115.  121.    6   5.93  118.  7.66  2.42  5.48
2 After   bp           10   111   135   120.  117.  127    9.75  6.67  122   7.50  2.37  5.36

> # Conduct t-test for paired samples
> bp_study %>%
+    t_test(bp ~ time, paired = TRUE, detailed = TRUE)

# A tibble: 1 x 13
  estimate .y.    group1 group2    n1    n2 statistic     p    df conf.low conf.high method  alternative
     <dbl> <chr>  <chr>  <chr>  <int> <int>     <dbl> <dbl> <dbl>    <dbl>     <dbl> <chr>   <chr>
*
1     -3.7 bp     Before After     10    10     -1.70 0.123     9    -8.62      1.22 T-test  two.sided
>
```

We see from this output that the mean systolic blood pressure was 118 before starting the medication and that it was 122 two weeks later. The value of the *t*-test statistic is 1.70 on 9 degrees of freedom, with $p =$ .123.

Base R Approach

We can conduct our paired samples *t*-test using a Base R approach by running the following code. The results are the same as those shown above, although the formatting is different.

```
# Get summary statistics
describe(bp_study$bp)
describeBy(bp_study$bp, bp_study$time)

# Conduct t-test for paired samples
t.test(bp ~ time, bp_study, paired = TRUE)
```

One-Way ANOVA

In this section we will take our first look at using R to conduct an analysis of variance (ANOVA), including an omnibus test and post-hoc tests (see Schochet, 2009, for a discussion of the important topic of controlling the Type I error rate). We will use data that could emerge from a study of the effect of three instructional methods (lecture, computer-assisted instruction (CAI), and a combination of lecture and computer-assisted instruction) on student math achievement (that is, grades), which are shown in Table 4.5.

We can create these data in Excel or use this code to create the dataframe inline using R code (I have named the data frame *math_study* and the variables *type* and *grade*):

```
type <- c("Lecture", "Lecture", "Lecture", "Lecture", "Lecture",
        "Lecture", "Lecture", "Lecture", "Lecture", "Lecture",
        "CAI", "CAI", "CAI", "CAI", "CAI",
        "CAI", "CAI", "CAI", "CAI", "CAI",
        "Combination", "Combination", "Combination", "Combination",
        "Combination", "Combination", "Combination", "Combination",
        "Combination", "Combination")
```

TABLE 4.5. Final Grade Data for Instructional Type

Lecture	CAI	CAI/lecture
80	84	90
82	86	92
78	84	94
76	82	90
80	88	100
72	90	94
82	92	94
88	88	96
74	86	92
68	84	94

Note. Terrell (2021, p. 261).

```
grade <- c(80, 82, 78, 76, 80, 72, 82, 88, 74, 68,
           84, 86, 84, 82, 88, 90, 92, 88, 86, 84,
           90, 92, 94, 90, 100, 94, 94, 96, 92, 94)
type <- factor(type)
math_study  <- data.frame(type, grade)
```

Tidyverse Approach

We will analyze these data in four steps, using functions from the *rstatix* package. We will first use the *get_summary_stats()* function to obtain descriptive statistics for the overall set of data, and then we will use that function again to obtain descriptive statistics for each of the three groups. Next, we will use the *anova_test()* function to obtain the ANOVA table. Finally, we will use the *pairwise_t_test()* function to conduct pairwise tests among the groups (using the Bonferroni procedure to control the Type I error rate). The following code accomplishes these tasks:

```
math_study %>%
   get_summary_stats()
math_study %>%
   group_by(type) %>%
   get_summary_stats()
math_study %>%
   anova_test(grade ~ type, detailed = TRUE)
math_study %>%
   pairwise_t_test(grade ~ type,
                   p.adjust.method = "bonferroni")
```

The results of the analysis are shown below. In particular, note the common descriptive statistics, the typical ANOVA table, as well as the generalized eta squared (labeled *ges*) measure of effect size and the table of pairwise tests showing the adjusted p-value. From the output we see that the mean grade was 86.4 for the group that received CAI instruction, 78.0 for the group that received lecture instruction, and 93.6 for the group that received combined instruction. The value of the F statistic is 35.719 on 2 and 27 degrees of freedom, with $p < .001$. The adjusted probabilities associated with the pairwise comparisons are $p = .002$ for CAI instruction versus combined instruction, $p < .001$ for CAI instruction versus lecture instruction, and $p < .001$ for lecture instruction versus combined instruction.

```
> math_study %>%
+   get_summary_stats()
# A tibble: 1 x 13
  variable      n   min   max median    q1    q3   iqr   mad  mean    sd    se    ci
  <chr>     <dbl> <dbl> <dbl>  <dbl> <dbl> <dbl> <dbl> <dbl> <dbl> <dbl> <dbl> <dbl>
1 grade        30    68   100     87    82    92    10  7.41    86  7.61  1.39  2.84

> math_study %>%
+   group_by(type) %>%
+   get_summary_stats()
# A tibble: 3 x 14
  type        variable     n   min   max median    q1    q3   iqr   mad  mean    sd    se    ci
  <fct>       <chr>    <dbl> <dbl> <dbl>  <dbl> <dbl> <dbl> <dbl> <dbl> <dbl> <dbl> <dbl> <dbl>
1 CAI         grade       10    82    92     86    84    88     4  2.96  86.4  3.10  0.98  2.22
2 Combination grade       10    90   100     94    92    94     2  2.96  93.6  2.95 0.933  2.11
3 Lecture     grade       10    68    88     79  74.5  81.5     7  4.45    78  5.74  1.81  4.10

> math_study %>%
+   anova_test(grade ~ type, detailed = TRUE)
Coefficient covariances computed by hccm()
ANOVA Table (type II tests)

  Effect    SSn   SSd DFn DFd      F       p p<.05   ges
1   type 1219.2 460.8   2  27 35.719 2.6e-08     * 0.726
> math_study %>%
+   pairwise_t_test(grade ~ type,
+                   p.adjust.method = "bonferroni")
# A tibble: 3 x 9
  .y.   group1      group2         n1    n2          p p.signif         p.adj p.adj.signif
* <chr> <chr>       <chr>       <int> <int>      <dbl> <chr>            <dbl> <chr>
1 grade CAI         Combination    10    10  0.000581  ***         0.00174   **
2 grade CAI         Lecture        10    10  0.000103  ***         0.000309  ***
3 grade Combination Lecture        10    10  0.00000000468 ****   0.0000000141 ****
```

Base R Approach

We can conduct our one-way ANOVA using a Base R approach by running the following code. The results are the same as those shown above, although the formatting is different.

```
# Get summary statistics
describe(math_study$grade)
describeBy(math_study$grade, math_study$type)

# Conduct the ANOVA and show the summary table
summary(aov(grade ~ type, math_study))

# Conduct the pairwise tests
pairwise.t.test(math_study$grade, math_study$type,
                p.adjust.method = "bonferroni")
```

Crosstabulation

In this section we look at crosstabulated data. The data we are analyzing may be in the form of raw data (that is, cases) or in the form of a contingency table of counts. If our data are in the form of cases, we can proceed with the crosstabulation; if they are in the form of a contingency table, we need to convert the table of counts to cases before running the crosstabulation. To see how to use data in the form of a contingency table of counts, we consider that data could emerge from a study of learning style and attrition in a distance learning environment. The data include two variables: *learning style* (classified based on responses to questions in a learning style inventory) and *status* (graduated or not graduated). These data are shown in Table 4.6 (the total number of students is 80).

We can use this R code to create a data frame that contains the data shown in the Table 4.6.:

```
# Create data table
dist_learn <- as.table(
  rbind(c(9, 16, 12, 10), c(5, 12, 6, 10)))
dimnames(dist_learn) <- list(
  Status = c("Graduate", "Non-graduate"),
  Learning_style = c("Accommodator", "Assimilator", "Diverger",
                     "Converger"))
dist_learn
```

Notice the use of the *as.table()* function to create the data table (named *dist_learn*), the *dimnames()* function to apply a set of labels to the dimensions of the table, and the *list()* function to create the list of labels. We can look at the table in the same way as any other R object, that is, by entering its name:

```
> # Create data table
> dist_learn <- as.table(
+   rbind(c(9, 16, 12, 10), c(5, 12, 6, 10)))
> dimnames(dist_learn) <- list(
+   Status = c("Graduate", "Non-graduate"),
+   Learning_style = c("Accommodator", "Assimilator", "Diverger",
+                      "Converger"))
> dist_learn
                Learning_style
Status           Accommodator Assimilator Diverger Converger
  Graduate                  9          16       12        10
  Non-graduate              5          12        6        10
```

TABLE 4.6.	Counts of Graduation Status within Learning Style			
	Learning style			
Status	Accommodator	Assimilator	Diverger	Converger
Graduate	9	16	12	10
Non-graduate	5	28	6	10
Note. Adapted from Terrell (2021, p. 328).				

Tidyverse Approach

We will again use the *rstatix* package to analyze these data. This time we will use the *chisq_test()* and *chisq_descriptives()* functions for our analysis. The following code will accomplish this task:

```
# Obtain the chi-square test statistic and probability
dist_learn %>%
  chisq_test()
# Obtain the chi-square details
dist_learn %>%
  chisq_test() %>%
  chisq_descriptives()
```

The results are shown below. In particular, note the observed cell frequencies (which match the data in Table 4.6), and the total, row, and column proportions (which you can multiply by 100 to obtain percentages). Given the layout of our data, we are interested in the column percentages (named *col.prop*), that is, the percentage who graduated within each learning style. From the *col.prop* column we see that among the Accommodators 64% gradated and 36% did not, among the Assimilators 57% gradated and 43% did not, among the Divergers 67% graduated and 33% did not, and among the Convergers 50% graduated and 50% did not. The value of the chi-square statistic is 1.30 on 3 degrees of freedom, with $p = .728$.

```
> # Obtain the chi-square test statistic and probability
> dist_learn %>%
+   chisq_test()
# A tibble: 1 x 6
      n statistic     p    df method          p.signif
* <dbl>     <dbl> <dbl> <int> <chr>           <chr>
1    80      1.30 0.728     3 Chi-square test ns

> # Obtain the chi-square details
> dist_learn %>%
```

```
+   chisq_test() %>%
+   chisq_descriptives()
# A tibble: 8 x 9
   Status       Learning_style observed  prop row.prop col.prop expected  resid std.resid
   <fct>        <fct>              <dbl> <dbl>    <dbl>    <dbl>    <dbl>  <dbl>     <dbl>
1 Graduate     Accomodator            9 0.112    0.191    0.643     8.22  0.270     0.463
2 Non-graduate Accomodator            5 0.0625   0.152    0.357     5.78 -0.322    -0.463
3 Graduate     Assimilator           16 0.2      0.340    0.571    16.4  -0.111    -0.214
4 Non-graduate Assimilator           12 0.15     0.364    0.429    11.6   0.132     0.214
5 Graduate     Diverger              12 0.15     0.255    0.667    10.6   0.438     0.775
6 Non-graduate Diverger               6 0.075    0.182    0.333     7.42 -0.523    -0.775
7 Graduate     Converger             10 0.125    0.213    0.5      11.8  -0.511    -0.918
8 Non-graduate Converger             10 0.125    0.303    0.5       8.25  0.609     0.918
```

Alternatively, we can use the *tabyl()* function from the *janitor* package and the *kable()* function from the *knitr* package to produce a more readable table, though we still need the *chisq_test()* function from the *rstatix* package to compute the test statistic. However, the *tabyl()* function expects a data frame of cases rather than a contingency table of counts (the format, for example, of our *example_data* data frame). Therefore, we will first use the *counts_to_cases()* function to create a data frame that we will then analyze with the *tabyl()* function.

```
library(janitor)
library(knitr)
# Convert counts to cases
dist_learn2 <- counts_to_cases(dist_learn)
# Create a table using the tabyl() and kable() functions
dist_learn2 %>%
    tabyl(Status, Learning_style) %>%
    adorn_totals(c("row", "col")) %>%
    adorn_percentages() %>%
    adorn_pct_formatting() %>%
    adorn_ns() %>%
    adorn_title() %>%
    kable()
# Run the chi-square test
dist_learn %>%
    chisq_test()
```

This code produces the following output.

```
> library(janitor)
> library(knitr)

> # Convert counts to cases
> dist_learn2 <- counts_to_cases(dist_learn)
```

```
> # Create a table using the tabyl() and kable() functions
> dist_learn2 %>%
+    tabyl(Status, Learning_style) %>%
+    adorn_totals(c("row", "col")) %>%
+    adorn_percentages() %>%
+    adorn_pct_formatting() %>%
+    adorn_ns() %>%
+    adorn_title() %>%
+    kable()
```

	|Learning_style					
Status	Accomodator	Assimilator	Diverger	Converger	Total
Graduate	19.1% (9)	34.0% (16)	25.5% (12)	21.3% (10)	100.0% (47)
Non-graduate	15.2% (5)	36.4% (12)	18.2% (6)	30.3% (10)	100.0% (33)
Total	17.5% (14)	35.0% (28)	22.5% (18)	25.0% (20)	100.0% (80)

```
> # Run the chi-square test
> dist_learn %>%
+    chisq_test()

# A tibble: 1 x 6
      n statistic     p    df method          p.signif
* <dbl>     <dbl> <dbl> <int> <chr>           <chr>
1    80      1.30 0.728     3 Chi-square test ns
```

Base R Approach

We can use the *CrossTable()* function from the *gmodels* package to obtain output that may be more familiar if you are accustomed to SPSS or SAS output. Like the *tabyl()* function, the *CrossTable()* function expects a data frame of cases rather than a contingency table of counts. The following code produces the crosstabulation (notice that several items have been set to *FALSE* so that they do not appear in the output and that an SPSS style output format has been selected):

```
# Load package
Library(gmodels)
# Obtain results using the CrossTable() function
CrossTable(dist_learn2$Learning_style, dist_learn2$Status,
           dnn = c("Program", "Satisfcation"),
           expected = FALSE, prop.c = FALSE, prop.t = FALSE,
           prop.chisq = FALSE, sresid = FALSE, chisq = TRUE,
           format = "SPSS")
```

The results are shown below, and match those we saw previously.

```
> # Obtain results using the CrossTable() function
> CrossTable(dist_learn2$Learning_style, dist_learn2$Status,
+          dnn = c("Program", "Satisfcation"),
+          expected = FALSE, prop.c = FALSE, prop.t = FALSE,
+          prop.chisq = FALSE, sresid = FALSE, chisq = TRUE,
+          format = "SPSS")


   Cell Contents
|-----------------------|
|                 Count |
|           Row Percent |
|-----------------------|


Total Observations in Table:   80


              | Satisfcation
     Program  |    Graduate  | Non-graduate  |   Row Total  |
-------------|--------------|---------------|--------------|
 Accomodator  |          9  |           5  |          14  |
              |    64.286%  |     35.714%  |     17.500%  |
-------------|--------------|---------------|--------------|
 Assimilator  |         16  |          12  |          28  |
              |    57.143%  |     42.857%  |     35.000%  |
-------------|--------------|---------------|--------------|
     Diverger  |         12  |           6  |          18  |
              |    66.667%  |     33.333%  |     22.500%  |
-------------|--------------|---------------|--------------|
    Converger  |         10  |          10  |          20  |
              |    50.000%  |     50.000%  |     25.000%  |
-------------|--------------|---------------|--------------|
 Column Total  |         47  |          33  |          80  |
-------------|--------------|---------------|--------------|


Statistics for All Table Factors


Pearson's Chi-squared test
------------------------------------------------------------
Chi^2 =  1.304228     d.f. =  3     p =  0.7281294


       Minimum expected frequency: 5.775
```

KEY TAKEAWAYS

Using R, we can accomplish many analytic tasks in several different ways. Use the way that that fits your context and style, and that provides you the output that you need.

In this chapter we used R to conduct common analyses, focusing on a small number of starting points.

You can build on the knowledge gained in this chapter to further develop your ability to use R and RStudio.

EXERCISES

1. The data in Table 4.7 represent anxiety scores for two groups of university students, some of whom participate in organized sports and some who do not (Terrell, 2021, p. 207). The researchers conducting the study hypothesize that the students who participate in organized sports will have lower levels of anxiety than those who do not. Find the mean and standard deviation for the two groups of students.

2. Use the data from Exercise 1 to conduct Levene's test and an independent samples *t*-test with a directional hypothesis.

3. The data in Table 4.8 show the time (in minutes) that elapsed between the time a pill was taken and the time headache symptoms were relieved, for three different pills (Terrell, 2021, p. 249). Conduct a one-way ANOVA to test whether there is a difference in time to relief among the three different pills.

TABLE 4.7. Anxiety Data

Students in organized sports			Students not in organized sports		
35	32	31	24	42	31
33	41	35	25	41	32
25	31	41	31	31	33
40	29	61	31	24	20
44	31	25	41	25	25

Note. Terrell (2021, p. 207).

TABLE 4.8. Amount of Time for Pill Type		
Pill 1	Pill 2	Pill 3
8	6	8
8	6	9
7	5	2
3	4	8
5	2	2

Note. From Terrell (2021, p. 249).

4. The data in Table 4.9 show grade distributions in a graduate school psychology class, for students whose undergraduate degree was in psychology and for students whose major was in other areas (Terrell, 2021, p. 331). Conduct a chi-square test to determine whether there is a relationship between major and grade.

TABLE 4.9. Counts of Grades within Major					
	Grade				
College major	A	B	C	D	F
Psychology	24	10	7	6	7
Other	10	15	13	11	12

Note. Numbers in the table represent counts of students (that is, counts of grades within major). Adapted from Terrell (2021, p. 331).

## CHAPTER 5

Factorial ANOVA, Repeated-Measures ANOVA, Correlation, and Regression

CHAPTER OBJECTIVES

▼ Continue building familiarity with using R to conduct analyses from both Tidyverse and Base R approaches.

▼ Conduct these analyses: factorial ANOVA, repeated-measures ANOVA, correlation, and regression.

▼ Continue developing facility in using R and RStudio through practice by carrying out the analyses in this chapter.

In this chapter we will continue using R to analyze data, building on the knowledge and skills we gained in the previous chapter. Our goal remains to further increase familiarity with R and RStudio and to further develop an ability to use them to carry out analytic tasks. In this chapter we will use R to conduct factorial ANOVA, repeated measures ANOVA, correlation, and regression. In doing so, we will blend Tidyverse and Base R approaches as we wish, without trying to remain strictly with one or the other. Since a given task can often be approached in several ways in R, the key point is to be flexible in our thinking as we figure out any particular data handling or analysis puzzle. Also, please keep in mind that a particular analysis procedure in R may or may not have the same default parameters that you are accustomed to, so it is worthwhile to peruse the relevant documentation. If feasible, it can be a good idea to check your analysis against previous work, work done concurrently using another software package, or an example worked in a textbook. The more familiar you become with using R, the less necessary that will be.

Factorial ANOVA

In this section we will look at a two-way factorial analysis of variance. The data arise from a study in which faculty members were concerned that an accrediting agency's mandate that technology be used at all levels of university instruction might affect the achievement of older students. A professor therefore arranged to teach two statistics classes in different ways: in one class, students used handheld calculators to work through the problems, and in the other class the students used personal computers in their work. The independent variables were *age* (30 years of age and younger, or over 30 years of age) and *technology type* (computers or calculators). The dependent variable was *achievement score* in the class. These data are shown in Table 5.1.

We can use this R code to create and look at the data frame (or we can enter them externally using Excel or some other software and then read that file):

```
# Create data frame
technology <- factor(rep(c("Computer", "Calculator"),
                         times = c(20, 20)))
age_group <- factor(rep(c("30 or younger", "Over 30",
                          "30 or younger", "Over 30"),
                        times = c(10, 10, 10, 10)))
score <- c(68, 67, 66, 73, 75, 69, 70, 71, 73, 74,
           79, 80, 76, 71, 72, 75, 75, 72, 71, 74,
           73, 73, 77, 77, 75, 77, 78, 69, 70, 71,
           70, 74, 75, 72, 72, 69, 73, 75, 76, 72)
tech_age <- data.frame(technology, age_group, score)
```

Notice the use of the *rep()* function to repeat a set of values the specified number of times. Also, notice that the order of the values matters, and the order they have been entered here is necessary to create a data frame that matches Table 5.1. We can look at the data frame in the

TABLE 5.1.	Score Data for Technology and Age Groups		
Technology	**Age group**	**Score**	
Computer	30 or younger	68	69
		67	70
		66	71
		73	73
		75	74
	Over 30	79	75
		80	75
		76	72
		71	71
		72	74
Calculator	30 or younger	73	77
		73	78
		77	69
		77	70
		75	71
	Over 30	70	69
		74	73
		75	75
		72	76
		72	72

Note. From Terrell (2021, p. 278).

same way as we can look at any other R object (for example, by entering its name or by using the *view()* function).

```
# Look at the data frame in the Console
tech_age
# View the data frame
view(tech_age)
```

Next, let's obtain the descriptive statistics. We would like to see the statistics for the overall group, for each technology type, for each age group, and for each combination of technology type and age group. We can use the following code to generate these results.

```
# Descriptive statistics for the entire group
tech_age %>%
  get_summary_stats(show = c("n", "min", "max", "median", "mean",
                             "sd", "se", "ci"))
# Descriptive statistics by techology type
tech_age %>%
  group_by(technology) %>%
  get_summary_stats(show = c("n", "min", "max", "median", "mean",
                             "sd", "se", "ci"))
# Descriptive statistics by age group
tech_age %>%
  group_by(age_group) %>%
  get_summary_stats(show = c("n", "min", "max", "median", "mean",
                             "sd", "se", "ci"))
# Descriptive statistics for each combination of technology type
and age group
tech_age %>%
  group_by(technology, age_group) %>%
  get_summary_stats(show = c("n", "min", "max", "median", "mean",
                             "sd", "se", "ci"))
```

The results from the previous lines of code are as follows.

```
> # Descriptive statistics for the entire group
> tech_age %>%
+   get_summary_stats(show = c("n", "min", "max", "median", "mean",
+                              "sd", "se", "ci"))
# A tibble: 1 x 9
  variable     n   min   max median  mean    sd    se    ci
  <chr>    <dbl> <dbl> <dbl>  <dbl> <dbl> <dbl> <dbl> <dbl>
1 score       40    66    80     73  73.0  3.24 0.512  1.04
> # Descriptive statistics by techology type
> tech_age %>%
+   group_by(technology) %>%
+   get_summary_stats(show = c("n", "min", "max", "median", "mean",
+                              "sd", "se", "ci"))
# A tibble: 2 x 10
  technology variable     n   min   max median  mean    sd    se    ci
  <fct>      <chr>    <dbl> <dbl> <dbl>  <dbl> <dbl> <dbl> <dbl> <dbl>
1 Calculator score       20    69    78     73  73.4  2.80 0.626  1.31
2 Computer   score       20    66    80   72.5  72.6  3.65 0.816  1.71
> # Descriptive statistics by age group
> tech_age %>%
+   group_by(age_group) %>%
+   get_summary_stats(show = c("n", "min", "max", "median", "mean",
+                              "sd", "se", "ci"))
# A tibble: 2 x 10
  age_group      variable     n   min   max median  mean    sd    se    ci
  <fct>          <chr>    <dbl> <dbl> <dbl>  <dbl> <dbl> <dbl> <dbl> <dbl>
```

```
1 30 or younger score        20    66    78    73    72.3  3.56 0.795  1.66
2 Over 30        score        20    69    80    73.5  73.6  2.82 0.629  1.32
> # Descriptive statistics for each combination of technology type and age group
> tech_age %>%
+   group_by(technology, age_group) %>%
+   get_summary_stats(show = c("n", "min", "max", "median", "mean",
+                     "sd", "se", "ci"))
# A tibble: 4 x 11
  technology age_group      variable    n   min   max median  mean    sd    se    ci
  <fct>      <fct>          <chr>    <dbl> <dbl> <dbl>  <dbl> <dbl> <dbl> <dbl> <dbl>
1 Calculator 30 or younger  score       10    69    78     74    74  3.27  1.03  2.34
2 Calculator Over 30        score       10    69    76   72.5  72.8  2.25 0.712  1.61
3 Computer   30 or younger  score       10    66    75   70.5  70.6  3.10  0.98  2.22
4 Computer   Over 30        score       10    71    80   74.5  74.5  3.17  1.00  2.27
```

Next, we will use the following lines of R code to run the ANOVA. We begin by using the *levene_test()* function from the *rstatix* package to test the assumption of equality of variances. Two ways of writing the line to conduct this test are shown, so that we can again show that there are often different ways we can instruct R to perform a given task. In this example, the second way has been commented out so that the procedure runs only once; we can remove the "#" at the beginning of line five if we wish to run the second way. We then use the *factorial_design()* function from the *rstatix* package to create an object that we use for our ANOVA; we pass to the function the name of our dataframe, dependent variable, and the between-subjects independent variables (as usual, you can enter the name of the object—tech_age_anova—to see what it contains). Finally, we use the *Anova()* function from the *car* package to run our ANOVA.

```
# Levene's test for homogeneity of variance
tech_age %>%
     levene_test(score ~ technology * age_group, center = mean)

# Levene's test for homogeneity of variance (alternative format for R code)
#levene_test(tech_age, score ~ technology * age_group, center = mean)

# Set up the ANOVA
tech_age_anova  <- factorial_design(tech_age, dv = score,
                                between = c(technology, age_group))
# Run the ANOVA
Anova(tech_age_anova$model, type = 3)
```

The results are shown in the following lines of code. The test statistic for Levene's test is 0.878 with $p = .462$. The results show a two-way interaction between type of technology used and age group (the F statistic is 7.35 on 1 and 36 degrees of freedom, and $p = .01$). Looking back at the output, we see that among those who were 30 years of age or younger, those who used a calculator (74.0) had a higher mean score than those who used a computer (70.6). In contrast, among those who were over 30 years of age, those who used a calculator (72.8) had a lower mean score than those who used a computer (74.5).

```
> # Levene's test for homogeneity of variance
> tech_age %>%
+    levene_test(score ~ technology * age_group, center = mean)
# A tibble: 1 x 4
    df1    df2 statistic      p
  <int>  <int>     <dbl>  <dbl>
1     3     36     0.878  0.462
> # Set up the ANOVA
> tech_age_anova  <- factorial_design(tech_age, dv = score,
+                              · between = c(technology, age_group))
> # Run the ANOVA
> Anova(tech_age_anova$model, type = 3)
Anova Table (Type III tests)
Response: score
                        Sum Sq Df   F value  Pr(>F)
(Intercept)             213014  1 24076.9385 < 2e-16 ***
technology                   7  1    0.8166 0.37217
age_group                   18  1    2.0600 0.15985
technology:age_group        65  1    7.3498 0.01021 *
Residuals                  318 36
---
Signif. codes:  0 '***' 0.001 '**' 0.01 '*' 0.05 '.' 0.1 ' ' 1
```

Repeated-Measures ANOVA

In this section will we will look at a repeated-measures ANOVA. Imagine a study in which participants were asked about their level of interest in a topic on three occasions. Their responses were rated on a 10-point scale, ranging from not at all interested (coded as *1*) to very interested (coded as *10*). These data are shown in Table 5.2.

Recalling the discussion of tidy data in Chapter 3, we can see that these data are not in a tidy format. That is, the variables *Time 1*, *Time 2*, and *Time 3* can be considered to represent one variable (*Time*) with three values (*1*, *2*, and *3*) rather than as three separate variables. If we read the data into a data frame using this *wide* format, we will need to reformat into a data frame with a *long* format before conducting our

		Rating	
Participant	**Time 1**	**Time 2**	**Time 3**
1	3	4	6
2	1	3	10
3	1	6	9
4	4	3	10
5	1	7	8
6	1	5	9
7	3	5	9
8	4	6	9
9	1	7	7
10	1	4	10

TABLE 5.2. Level of Interest in a Topic Rated on Three Occasions

repeated measures ANOVA. This is how it may come to you if you are receiving data from someone else, unless you have asked them to send it to you in long format. You can use the following R code to enter the data in wide format (of course, you could also enter it in long format and thereby save the reformatting step):

```
# Create the data frame
participant <- rep(1:10)
time1 <- c(3, 1, 1, 4, 1, 1, 3, 4, 1, 1)
time2 <- c(4, 3, 6, 3, 7, 5, 5, 6, 7, 4)
time3 <- c(6, 10, 9, 10, 8, 9, 9, 9, 7, 10)
interest <- data.frame(participant, time1, time2, time3)
```

Next, we use the *pivot_longer()* function to reformat the data from wide to long, and then we view both dataframes to check our work:

```
# Reformat the data
interest_long <- interest %>%
  pivot_longer(c(time1, time2, time3),
          names_to = "time", values_to = "interest")

# View the data
interest
interest_long
```

This code produces the following result.

```
> # Reformat the data
> interest_long <- interest %>%
+    pivot_longer(c(time1, time2, time3),
+                 names_to = "time", values_to = "interest")
> # View the data
> interest
  participant time1 time2 time3
1            1     3     4     6
2            2     1     3    10
3            3     1     6     9
4            4     4     3    10
5            5     1     7     8
6            6     1     5     9
7            7     3     5     9
8            8     4     6     9
9            9     1     7     7
10          10     1     4    10
> interest_long
# A tibble: 30 x 3
   participant time   interest
         <int> <chr>     <dbl>
1            1 time1         3
2            1 time2         4
3            1 time3         6
4            2 time1         1
5            2 time2         3
6            2 time3        10
7            3 time1         1
8            3 time2         6
9            3 time3         9
10           4 time1         4
# ... with 20 more rows
```

Now we are ready to conduct the repeated measures ANOVA. We will first obtain the descriptive statistics (though not necessary, we will look at descriptive statistics from both the original file and the reformatted formatted file to illustrate that they are the same). We will then again use the *factorial_design()* function from the *rstatix* package to create an object that we will use for our repeated measures ANOVA. We pass to the function the name of our dataframe, the dependent variable, the variable that identifies each subject (*participant* in this example), and the within-subjects variable (*time* in this example). Finally, we use the *Anova()* function from the *car* package to run our ANOVA and then follow up with pairwise comparisons. The following R code accomplishes this task, starting with obtaining the descriptive statistics:

```
# Descriptive statistics from the original data frame
interest %>%
  get_summary_stats(time1, time2, time3,
                    show = c("n", "min", "max", "median", "mean",
                             "sd", "se", "ci"))
# Descriptive statistics from the reformatted data frame
interest_long %>%
  group_by(time) %>%
  get_summary_stats(interest,
                    show = c("n", "min", "max", "median", "mean",
                             "sd", "se", "ci"))
```

The results from the descriptive procedures are shown below.

```
> # Descriptive statistics from the original data frame
> interest %>%
+   get_summary_stats(time1, time2, time3,
+                     show = c("n", "min", "max", "median", "mean",
+                              "sd", "se", "ci"))
# A tibble: 3 x 9
  variable     n   min   max median  mean    sd    se    ci
  <chr>    <dbl> <dbl> <dbl>  <dbl> <dbl> <dbl> <dbl> <dbl>
1 time1       10     1     4      1     2  1.33 0.422 0.954
2 time2       10     3     7      5     5  1.49 0.471 1.07
3 time3       10     6    10      9   8.7  1.34 0.423 0.957
> # Descriptive statistics from the reformatted data frame
> interest_long %>%
+   group_by(time) %>%
+   get_summary_stats(interest,
+                     show = c("n", "min", "max", "median", "mean",
+                              "sd", "se", "ci"))
# A tibble: 3 x 10
  time  variable     n   min   max median  mean    sd    se    ci
  <chr> <chr>    <dbl> <dbl> <dbl>  <dbl> <dbl> <dbl> <dbl> <dbl>
1 time1 interest    10     1     4      1     2  1.33 0.422 0.954
2 time2 interest    10     3     7      5     5  1.49 0.471 1.07
3 time3 interest    10     6    10      9   8.7  1.34 0.423 0.957
```

Next, we set up the ANOVA using the *factorial_design()* function to create an object (here called *stsfactn_design*) and providing the name of the data frame (*stsfctn_long*), the dependent variable (*satisfaction*), the variable that identifies the cases (*participant*), and the within-subjects variable (*time*). We then use the *Anova()* function to create an object (*stsfctn_rptdanova*) that contains the results of the analysis, and then display the results in an ANOVA table by entering the name of the object. We can also use the *summary()* function to show more details from the analysis (including Mauchly's test of sphericity).

```
# Set up the repeated measures ANOVA
interest_design <- factorial_design(interest_long, dv = interest,
                                    wid = participant, within = time)
# Conduct the repeated measures ANOVA
interest_rptdanova <- Anova(interest_design$model,
                            idata = interest_design$idata,
                            idesign = interest_design$idesign, type = 3)
# Show the repeated measures ANOVA table
interest_rptdanova
# Show detailed results from the repeated measures ANOVA
summary(interest_rptdanova)
```

The results are shown below, and we can see that there is an overall effect for time (the Wilk's lambda statistic = .07) and an approximate F value of 58.02 on 2 and 8 degrees of freedom, with $p <.001$).

```
> # Set up the repeated measures ANOVA
> interest_design <- factorial_design(interest_long, dv = interest,
+                                     wid = participant, within = time)
> # Conduct the repeated measures ANOVA
> interest_rptdanova <- Anova(interest_design$model,
+                             idata = interest_design$idata,
+                             idesign = interest_design$idesign, type = 3)
> # Show the repeated measures ANOVA table
> interest_rptdanova
Type III Repeated Measures MANOVA Tests: Pillai test statistic
            Df test stat approx F num Df den Df    Pr(>F)
(Intercept)  1   0.98952   849.97      1      9 3.205e-10 ***
time         1   0.93335    56.02      2      8 1.973e-05 ***
---
Signif. codes:  0 '***' 0.001 '**' 0.01 '*' 0.05 '.' 0.1 ' ' 1
> # Show detailed results from repeated measures ANOVA
> summary(interest_rptdanova)

Type III Repeated Measures MANOVA Tests:
------------------------------------------
Term: (Intercept)
 Response transformation matrix:
      (Intercept)
time1           1
time2           1
time3           1
```

```
Sum of squares and products for the hypothesis:
          (Intercept)
(Intercept)     2464.9


Multivariate Tests: (Intercept)
                Df test stat approx F num Df den Df    Pr(>F)
Pillai           1  0.98952 849.9655        1      9 3.2052e-10 ***
Wilks            1  0.01048 849.9655        1      9 3.2052e-10 ***
Hotelling-Lawley 1 94.44061 849.9655        1      9 3.2052e-10 ***
Roy              1 94.44061 849.9655        1      9 3.2052e-10 ***
---
Signif. codes:  0 '***' 0.001 '**' 0.01 '*' 0.05 '.' 0.1 ' ' 1


----------------------------------------


Term: time

 Response transformation matrix:
      time1 time2
time1     1     0
time2     0     1
time3    -1    -1

Sum of squares and products for the hypothesis:
      time1 time2
time1 448.9 247.9
time2 247.9 136.9


Multivariate Tests: time

                Df test stat approx F num Df den Df    Pr(>F)
Pillai           1 0.933354 56.01835        2      8 1.9729e-05 ***
Wilks            1 0.066646 56.01835        2      8 1.9729e-05 ***
Hotelling-Lawley 1 14.004589 56.01835       2      8 1.9729e-05 ***
Roy              1 14.004589 56.01835       2      8 1.9729e-05 ***
---
Signif. codes:  0 '***' 0.001 '**' 0.01 '*' 0.05 '.' 0.1 ' ' 1

Univariate Type III Repeated-Measures ANOVA Assuming Sphericity

            Sum Sq num Df Error SS den Df F value    Pr(>F)
(Intercept) 821.63      1      8.7      9 849.966 3.205e-10 ***
time        225.27      2     43.4     18  46.714 7.490e-08 ***
---
Signif. codes:  0 '***' 0.001 '**' 0.01 '*' 0.05 '.' 0.1 ' ' 1


Mauchly Tests for Sphericity

     Test statistic p-value
time       0.92562 0.73407
```

```
Greenhouse-Geisser and Huynh-Feldt Corrections
 for Departure from Sphericity

      GG eps Pr(>F[GG])
time 0.93077   1.94e-07 ***
---
Signif. codes:  0 '***' 0.001 '**' 0.01 '*' 0.05 '.' 0.1 ' ' 1


      HF eps   Pr(>F[HF])
time 1.163798 7.490029e-08
Warning message:
In summary.Anova.mlm(interest_rptdanova) : HF eps > 1 treated as 1
```

Finally, we use the following R code to conduct the follow-up pairwise comparisons.

```
# Conduct pairwise tests
stsfctn_long %>%
  pairwise_t_test(
    satisfaction ~ time, paired = TRUE,
    p.adjust.method = "holm")
```

The results are shown below, where we see that for the comparison between Time 1 and Time 2 the adjusted $p = .002$; for the comparison between Time 1 and Time 3 the adjusted $p < .001$; and for the comparison between Time 2 and Time 3 the adjusted $p = .002$.

```
> # Conduct pairwise tests
> interest_long %>%
+   pairwise_t_test(
+     interest ~ time, paired = TRUE,
+     p.adjust.method = "holm")
# A tibble: 3 x 10
  .y.       group1 group2    n1    n2 statistic    df          p       p.adj p.adj.signif
* <chr>     <chr>  <chr>  <int> <int>     <dbl> <dbl>      <dbl>       <dbl> <chr>
1 interest  time1  time2     10    10     -4.20     9 0.002          0.002        **
2 interest  time1  time3     10    10    -11.2      9 0.00000136     0.00000408   ****
3 interest  time2  time3     10    10     -4.86     9 0.000892       0.002        **
```

Correlation

In this section we will look at bivariate correlation. The variables include the number of times students were absent from a class during a semester and their score on a final exam. We are interested in the correlation between these two variables. These data are shown in Table 5.3.

TABLE 5.3. **Absences and Score Data**

Absences	Score	Absences	Score	Absences	Score	Absences	Score
1	100	4	85	7	70	12	70
2	95	6	82	9	90	6	80
4	90	7	80	11	55	7	80
5	90	2	97	2	94	2	93
6	80	7	77	1	90	3	88

Note. From Terrell (2021, p. 348).

We can use this R code to create and look at the data frame (or we can enter them externally using Excel or some other software and then read that file):

```
# Create the data frame
absences <- c(1, 2, 4, 5, 6, 4, 6, 7, 2, 7,
              7, 9, 11, 2, 1, 12, 6, 7, 2,3)
score <- c(100, 95, 90, 90, 80, 85, 82, 80, 97, 77,
           70, 90, 55, 94, 90, 70, 80, 80, 93, 88)
go_to_class <- data.frame(absences, score)

# Look at the data frame
go_to_class
```

Let's obtain descriptive statistics for these two variables, the correlation between them, and the probability associated with that correlation. We can use this R code to obtain these results:

```
# Descriptive statistics
go_to_class %>%
  describe()

# Obtain the correlation and its probability
cor.test(go_to_class$absences, go_to_class$score)
```

The results are shown below. Note that the default for this function is to compute Pearson's product-moment correlation. If more appropriate for your data (for example, if you are correlating ranked data), you can obtain Kendall's Tau or Spearman's Rho by instructing the *cor. test()* function to use either of those methods. The format for specifying a method is *cor.test(variable1, variable2, method = "method")*, where "*method*" is either "*spearman*" or "*kendall.*" From this output we see that the mean number of absences is 5.2 (with a standard deviation of 3.2), the mean score is 84.3 (with a standard deviation of 10.9), and the correlation between these two variables is –.84 with $p < .001$.

```
> # Descriptive statistics
> go_to_class %>%
+    describe()
           vars  n mean     sd median trimmed  mad min max range  skew kurtosis   se
absences     1 20  5.2  3.19    5.5    4.94 2.97   1  12    11  0.46    -0.78 0.71
score        2 20 84.3 10.85   86.5   85.25 9.64  55 100    45 -0.87     0.41 2.43
> # Obtain the correlation and its probability
> cor.test(go_to_class$absences, go_to_class$score)

        Pearson's product-moment correlation

data:  go_to_class$absences and go_to_class$score
t = -6.4522, df = 18, p-value = 4.524e-06
alternative hypothesis: true correlation is not equal to 0
95 percent confidence interval:
 -0.9330692 -0.6236036
sample estimates:
       cor
-0.8355485
```

We commonly want to visualize a correlation between variables by drawing a scatterplot. We will explore using R for data visualization in the next chapter, with a focus on the *ggplot2()* package. For now, though, let's obtain an scatterplot using the *plot()* function. At its simplest, we can write *plot(x, y)*, for example:

```
plot(go_to_class$score, go_to_class$absences)
```

Running this code will produce a scatterplot that is shown in the *Plots* tab of the bottom right pane in RStudio. We can improve this scatterplot by adjusting the X and Y axis limits, choosing a different plot symbol, adding a title, and adding X and Y axis labels (we could also add a regression line, as described in the next section). The following R code accomplishes these tasks (notice that the comments are used in the same lines as code, as an alternative to having them on separate lines):

```
plot(go_to_class$score, go_to_class$absences,    # Variables to plot
     xlim = c(50, 110),                           # Set X axis limits
     ylim = c(0, 14),                             # Set Y axis limits
```

```
pch = 16,                                    # Set plot symbol
col = "black",                               # Set symbol color
main = "Scatterplot of Absences and Score on Final Exam", # Main title
xlab = "Score",                              # X axis label
ylab = "Absences")                           # Y axis label
```

The resulting scatterplot is shown in Figure 5.1.

Regression

In this section we will first use R to conduct a simple regression analysis, and then we will build on that foundation to conduct a multiple regression analysis.

Simple Regression

In this section we use the *lm()* function to fit a linear regression model. We use the *age* and *accident* data in the following table to examine the relationship between a driver's *age* and the number of automobile *accidents* they are involved in during a given year. We will set up the model so that the number of *accidents* is predicted based on *age*. For our analysis, we will want the descriptive statistics for the two variables, the correlation between them, the regression equation, and a scatterplot of the two variables along with the regression line. The data are shown in Table 5.4.

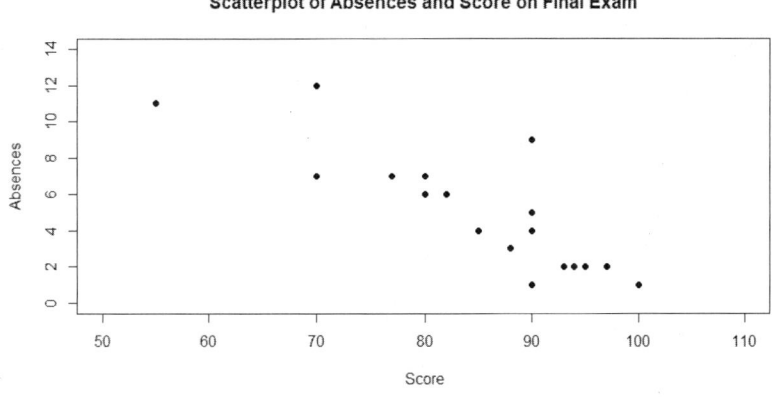

FIGURE 5.1. Scatterplot.

TABLE 5.4. Age and Accident Data							
Age	Accidents	Age	Accidents	Age	Accidents	Age	Accidents
67	4	66	4	82	3	85	2
72	3	82	0	83	2	76	4
65	6	79	2	70	5	65	3
78	2	77	5	73	4	74	3
80	1	73	3	67	5	79	3

Note. From Terrell (2021, p. 368).

We can use this R code to create and look at the data frame (or we can enter the data externally using Excel or some other software and then read that file):

```
age <- c(67, 72, 65, 78, 80, 66, 82, 79, 77, 73,
        82, 83, 70, 73, 67, 85, 76, 65,74, 79)
accidents <- c(4, 3, 6, 2, 1, 4, 0, 2, 5, 3,
              3, 2, 5, 4, 5, 2, 4, 3, 3, 3)
driving <- data.frame(age, accidents)
driving
```

Now, let's obtain descriptive statistics for these two variables, the correlation between them and the probability associated with that correlation, and the regression equation. The general format of the *lm()* function is *lm(y ~ x, dataframe)*, where *y* is the criterion (dependent variable) and *x* is the predictor (independent variable). We also use the *summary()* function to display details that are otherwise not displayed (we can run this *lm()* function with and without the *summary()* function to see the difference). We can use this R code to obtain these results:

```
# Descriptive statistics
driving %>%
  describe
# Correlation and its probability
cor.test(driving$age, driving$accidents)
# Obtain the linear model and display the results
lm(accidents ~ age, driving) %>%
  summary()
# Alternative coding to obtain the linear model and display the results
#summary(lm(accidents ~ age, driving))
```

The results are shown below. The F statistic for the model is 16.72 on 1 and 18 degrees of freedom, with $p < .001$. The multiple R-squared is .48. For the age variable, the t-statistic is –4.09 with $p < .001$. The regression equation is: $\hat{Y} = 15.09 - 0.16(age)$.

```
> # Descriptive statistics
> driving %>%
+   describe
          vars  n  mean   sd median trimmed  mad min max range  skew kurtosis   se
age          1 20 74.65 6.42     75   74.69 7.41  65  85    20 -0.12    -1.40 1.44
accidents    2 20  3.20 1.47      3    3.25 1.48   0   6     6 -0.14    -0.54 0.33
> # Correlation and its probability
> cor.test(driving$age, driving$accidents)

        Pearson's product-moment correlation

data:  driving$age and driving$accidents
t = -4.0887, df = 18, p-value = 0.0006893
alternative hypothesis: true correlation is not equal to 0
95 percent confidence interval:
 -0.8694570 -0.3628188
sample estimates:
       cor
-0.6939264


> # Obtain the linear model and display the results
> lm(accidents ~ age, driving) %>%
+   summary()

Call:
lm(formula = accidents ~ age, data = driving)

Residuals:
    Min      1Q  Median      3Q     Max
-2.02971 -0.58844 -0.08699  0.67903  2.17417

Coefficients:
            Estimate Std. Error t value Pr(>|t|)
(Intercept) 15.08600    2.91720   5.171 6.42e-05 ***
age         -0.15922    0.03894  -4.089 0.000689 ***
---
Signif. codes:  0 '***' 0.001 '**' 0.01 '*' 0.05 '.' 0.1 ' ' 1

Residual standard error: 1.089 on 18 degrees of freedom
Multiple R-squared:  0.4815, Adjusted R-squared:  0.4527
F-statistic: 16.72 on 1 and 18 DF,  p-value: 0.0006893
```

In addition to the code above, we can obtain information from the regression analysis using functions from the *moderndive* package, including *get_regression_table()*, *get_regression_summaries()*, and *get_regression_points()*. Give these a try to see how their output is similar or different.

```
# Obtain results from the moderndive package
library(moderndive)
lm(accidents ~ age, driving) %>%
  get_regression_table()
lm(accidents ~ age, driving) %>%
  get_regression_summaries()
lm(accidents ~ age, driving) %>%
  get_regression_points()
```

We can use the following R code to visualize the results of the regression by drawing a scatterplot and then superimposing the regression line. We will again use the *plot()* function to draw the scatterplot, and then we will use the *abline()* function to draw the regression line. Note that the *abline()* function operates on the same *lm()* function that we just used for the regression equation; also note that the order of the variables is different in the *plot()* and *abline()* functions.

```
plot(driving$age, driving$accidents,            # Variables to plot
     xlim = c(60, 90),                          # Set X axis limits
     ylim = c(0, 7),                            # Set Y axis limits
     pch = 16,                                  # Set plot symbol
     col = "black",                             # Set symbol color
     main = "Scatterplot of Age and Accidents", # Main title
     xlab = "Age",                              # X axis label
     ylab = "Accidents")                        # Y axis label
abline(lm(accidents ~ age, driving))
```

The scatterplot is shown in Figure 5.2.

Multiple Regression

Hayes (2022) thoroughly explores a regression approach to mediation and moderation analysis, in part using a data set that examines the extent to which "people's beliefs about the role government should play in mitigating the potential effects of a global crisis related to their emotional reactions to such a crisis" (p. 30). This data set (named GLBWARM)

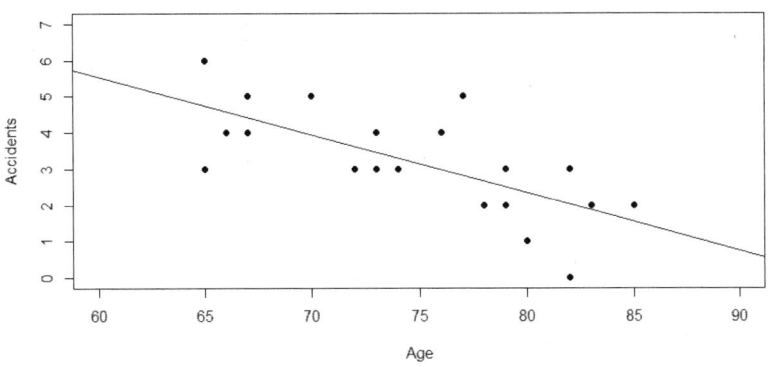

FIGURE 5.2. Scatterplot with regression line.

is available from the book's companion website.[1] We will use it to run a multiple regression with the following variables:

GOVACT: index of support for government action to reduce climate change (an average across five questions about the extent to which the respondent supports various policies or actions, scaled "strongly opposed" coded as *1* to "strongly support" coded as *7*);

NEGEMOT: index of negative emotions about climate change (an average across three questions about how frequently the respondent feels "worried," "alarmed," and "concerned" about global warming, scaled from "not at all" coded as *1* to "a great deal" coded as *6*);

POSEMOT: index of positive emotions about climate change (an average across three questions about how frequently the respondent feels "hopeful," "encouraged," and "optimistic" about global climate change, scaled from "not at all" coded as *1* to "a great deal" coded as *6*);

IDEOLOGY: respondent's rating of their political ideology (on a scale of "very liberal" coded as *1* to "very conservative" coded as *7*);

---

[1] *http://afhayes.com/introduction-to-mediation-moderation-and-conditional-process-analysis.html.*

SEX: respondent's sex ("female" coded as *0* or "male" coded as *1*);

AGE: respondent's age at last birthday.

We can use the following R code to conduct this analysis. First, read the data file. If the data file is in your current project directory, you do not need to include the *pathname*. If you do need to include a pathname, remember to use the forward slash ("/") rather than the backslash in the name. Next, we use the *describe ()* function to obtain the descriptive statistics. Then we use the *lm()* function to run the multiple regression and create an object (I have called it *gwarmMultipleReg*) to hold the results from the multiple regression. Notice that the format for the multiple regression is similar to the format for the simple regression above, and we have just added more terms. Finally, use the *aov()* function (another analysis of variance function) to obtain the sum of squares and degrees of freedom; the *summary()* function to obtain the regression coefficients, R-squared and adjusted R-squared, and the F test for the regression model and its associated probability; and the *confint()* function to obtain the confidence intervals for the regression coefficients.

```
# Read data file
glbwarm <- read_csv("pathname/glbwarm.csv")
# Descriptive statistics
glbwarm %>%
  describe()
# Create an object with the results of the multiple regression
gwarmMultipleReg <- lm(govact ~ negemot + posemot + ideology + sex + age,
                  data = glbwarm)
# Sum of squares and degrees of freedom
aov(gwarmMultipleReg)
# Regression coefficients, R-squared and adjusted R-squared,
#    F test of the regression model and associated probability
summary(gwarmMultipleReg)
# Confidence intervals for the regression coefficients
confint(gwarmMultipleReg)
```

The results are shown below. The F statistic for the model is 102.7 on 5 and 809 degrees of freedom, with $p < .001$. The multiple R-squared is .38. For the age variable, the t-statistic is −4.09 with $p < .001$. The regression equation is: $\hat{Y} = 4.064 + 0.441(\text{negemot}) − .0.027(\text{posemot}) − 0.21 (\text{ideology}) − 0.10 (\text{sex}) − 0.001 (\text{age})$.

```
> # Descriptive statistics
> glbwarm %>%
+     describe()
         vars   n  mean    sd median trimmed   mad min max range  skew kurtosis   se
govact      1 815  4.59  1.36   4.80    4.68  1.19   1   7     6 -0.63     0.22 0.05
posemot     2 815  3.13  1.35   3.00    3.11  1.48   1   6     5  0.09    -0.85 0.05
negemot     3 815  3.56  1.53   3.67    3.58  1.97   1   6     5 -0.15    -1.07 0.05
ideology    4 815  4.08  1.51   4.00    4.07  1.48   1   7     6  0.03    -0.43 0.05
age         5 815 49.54 16.33  51.00   49.66 19.27  17  87    70 -0.07    -1.03 0.57
sex         6 815  0.49  0.50   0.00    0.49  0.00   0   1     1  0.05    -2.00 0.02
partyid     7 815  1.88  0.87   2.00    1.85  1.48   1   3     2  0.23    -1.63 0.03
> # Create an object with the results of the multiple regression
> gwarmMultipleReg <- lm(govact ~ negemot + posemot + ideology + sex + age,
+                         data = glbwarm)
> # Sum of squares and degrees of freedom
> aov(gwarmMultipleReg)
Call:
   aov(formula = gwarmMultipleReg)

Terms:
                 negemot  posemot ideology      sex      age Residuals
Sum of Squares  502.8690   1.4603  80.2918   0.0505   0.3472  921.5233
Deg. of Freedom        1        1        1        1        1       809

Residual standard error: 1.067281
Estimated effects may be unbalanced
> # Regression coefficients, R-squared and adjusted R-squared,
> #    F test of the regression model and associated probability
> summary(gwarmMultipleReg)

Call:
lm(formula = govact ~ negemot + posemot + ideology + sex + age,
    data = glbwarm)

Residuals:
    Min      1Q  Median      3Q     Max
-4.8381 -0.6834  0.0705  0.7008  3.4266

Coefficients:
             Estimate Std. Error t value Pr(>|t|)
(Intercept)  4.063607   0.205323  19.791  < 2e-16 ***
negemot      0.440781   0.026433  16.676  < 2e-16 ***
posemot     -0.026778   0.028145  -0.951    0.342
ideology    -0.218269   0.027043  -8.071 2.51e-15 ***
sex         -0.010066   0.076743  -0.131    0.896
age         -0.001309   0.002371  -0.552    0.581
---
Signif. codes:  0 '***' 0.001 '**' 0.01 '*' 0.05 '.' 0.1 ' ' 1

Residual standard error: 1.067 on 809 degrees of freedom
Multiple R-squared:  0.3883,     Adjusted R-squared:  0.3845
F-statistic: 102.7 on 5 and 809 DF,  p-value: < 2.2e-16

> # Confidence intervals for the regression coefficients
> confint(gwarmMultipleReg)
                  2.5 %       97.5 %
(Intercept) 3.660577619  4.466635415
```

```
negemot      0.388896210   0.492665216
posemot     -0.082024253   0.028468841
ideology    -0.271352089  -0.165185612
sex         -0.160705662   0.140573228
age         -0.005962039   0.003344543
```

As before, we can use the functions in the *moderndive* package to obtain this information (give it a try and compare the output with that shown above):

```
gwarmMultipleReg %>%
  get_regression_table()
gwarmMultipleReg %>%
  get_regression_summaries()
gwarmMultipleReg %>%
  get_regression_points()
```

KEY TAKEAWAYS

- As in the previous chapter, we continue to see that many analytic tasks can be accomplished in several different ways. Use the way that fits your context and style and that provides the output you need.

- In this chapter we used R to conduct additional common analyses, focusing on a small number of starting points.

- You can continue to build on the knowledge gained in this chapter to further develop your ability to use R and RStudio.

EXERCISES

1. The data in Table 5.5 represent tuition reimbursement spent by a company during a given year and the number of resignations during that same year (company management was concerned that more and more employees were taking the benefit, becoming better educated, and moving to another company for a higher salary (Terrell, 2021, p. 336). Display the variables in a scatterplot and the Pearson correlation coefficient.

2. Add the regression line to the scatterplot created in Exercise 1.

3. Analyze the data in Exercise 1 using linear regression.

TABLE 5.5. Tuition and Resignations by Year

Year	Tuition (thousands of dollars)	Resignations
1	32	20
2	38	25
3	41	28
4	42	25
5	50	30
6	60	32
7	57	40
8	70	45
9	80	45
10	100	90

Note. From Terrell (2021, p. 336).

CHAPTER 6

Data Visualization

▼ CHAPTER OBJECTIVES

▽ Become familiar with the fundamentals of the layered grammar of graphics.

▽ Become familiar with the *ggplot()* function from the *ggplot2* package, and use it to draw a variety of graphs.

R is noted for its remarkable ability to produce data visualizations. This chapter begins with a brief discussion of the layered grammar of graphics, which can be used to understand the underlying structure of any graph. As noted by Wickham (2010), "A grammar of graphics is a tool that enables us to concisely describe the components of a graphic. Such a grammar allows us to move beyond named graphics (e.g., the "scatterplot") and gain insight into the deep structure that underlies statistical graphics" (p. 3).

The chapter then introduces the *ggplot2* package, which uses the layered grammar of graphics[1] to provide users with tremendous flexibility in creating data visualizations. Many other functions in R can be used for creating graphics. For example, we used the *plot()* function in

---

[1] See Wickham, Navarro, and Pedersen (*https://ggplot2-book.org*) for a detailed explanation of the grammar of graphics.

the previous chapter to draw a scatterplot. Sometimes during our work when we want to take a quick look at our data, a simple function like *plot()* may be sufficient. As another example, in the next section we will briefly look at the *histogram()* function. However, our focus will be on the *ggplot2* package, since it is part of the Tidyverse and has considerable capability.

Layered Grammar of Graphics

Among the many brilliant aspects of R is the *ggplot2* package, which we can use to create data visualizations from the point of view of the layered grammar of graphics. Let's explore the fundamentals of this grammar. We begin by considering the example graph in Figure 6.1.

In order to create this graph, we start with some data. Here we have hypothetical data about respondents' level of patience during a learning task (from *low* coded as *1* to *high* coded as 5). Next, we transform the data into the information we want to display (in this graph we have transformed the raw data into percentages). We then choose a

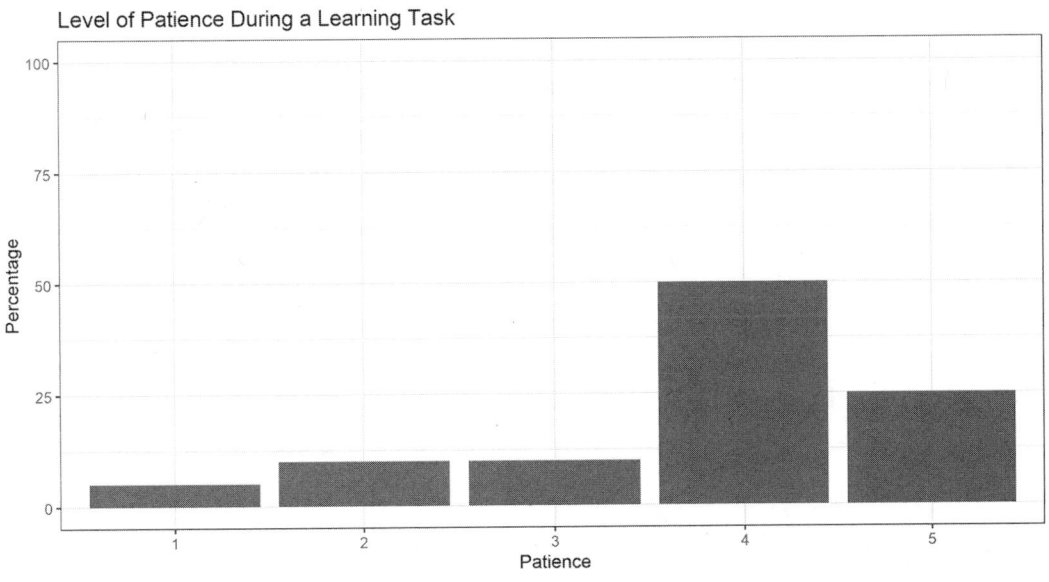

FIGURE 6.1. Example graph.

geometric object to represent the transformed data (here we have chosen bars), use aesthetic properties of the object to represent variables (here the bars represent the *Patience* variable), and map the values of the variable to the levels of the aesthetic (here the height of the bar represents the percentage for each patience rating). Finally, we place the geometric object onto a coordinate system (here we have levels of patience on the X axis and percentage on the Y axis). In brief, what we have done is:

- Started with a data set,
- Transformed the data into the information to display (in *ggplot()*, a "*stat*"),
- Chosen a geometric object to represent the transformed data (in *ggplot()*, a "*geom*"),
- Used aesthetic properties of the geometric object to represent variables (in *ggplot()*, an "*aes*"),
- Mapped the values of each variable to the levels of the aesthetic, and
- Placed the geometric objects onto a coordinate system.

The brilliance and beauty of the layered grammar of graphics is that we can use it to create any plot that we can imagine. We explore this matter further in the rest of this chapter. Be sure to work with the code as we go along so that you become familiar with it and gain an understanding of how it works.

Bar Chart

Let's begin by creating the example graph shown above. Our data set contains three variables: ID is a unique identifier for each case, *Patience* is the respondents' rating of their level of patience during a learning task (from *low* coded as *1* to *high* coded as *5*), and *Group* is an indicator of group membership (coded as *1* or *2*). The following R code creates this data frame, displays the data frame in the Console, provides an overall frequency distribution for the *Patience* variable, and presents a frequency distribution for the *Patience* variable for each *Group*:

```
# Create variables
ID <- c(1:20)
Group <- factor(rep(c(1, 2), times = c(10, 10)))
Patience <- c(4, 3, 3, 4, 4, 5, 2, 4, 4, 1, 4, 5, 4, 5, 4, 4, 5, 4, 5, 2)
# Create data frame
patience_data <- data.frame(ID, Patience, Group)
# Display data frame
patience_data
# Create overall frequency distribution
patience_data %>%
  group_by(Patience) %>%
  summarize(N = n()) %>%
  mutate(Percent = prop.table(N) * 100)
# Create frequency distribution by group
patience_data %>%
  group_by(Group, Patience) %>%
  summarize(N = n()) %>%
  mutate(Percent = prop.table(N) * 100)
```

First, we will use the *hist()* function to create a frequency distribution for the Patience variable, and the *histogram()* function to display a graph of percentages rather than frequencies. The following lines of code will produce these two basic graphs:

```
hist(patience_data$Patience)
histogram(patience_data$Patience)
```

We can modify elements of the graphs produced by these functions, if we wish. For example, we can add a title, change the X axis label, Y axis limits, and color of the bars, using the following lines of code:

```
hist(patience_data$Patience,
     main = "Level of Patience During a Learning Task",
     xlab = "Patience",
     ylim = c(0, 15),
     col = "gray")
```

R includes 657 colors we can choose from, which we can see using the *colors()* function:

```
colors()
```

Let's now use the *ggplot2* package to create a bar chart for the *Patience* variable. The following R code gets us started (remember to first load the *Tidyverse* package if you have not already done so during this R session):

```
patience_data %>%
  ggplot(mapping = aes(x = Patience)) +
  geom_bar()
```

Notice that in this code we have:

- Read the (*patience_data*) data frame,
- Called the *ggplot()* function and transformed the data into the information to display (the default for *geom_bar()* is to use *stat_count()* in order to count the number of cases for each value of the variable *Patience*, so we did not have to specify that in this code),
- Used aesthetic properties of the geometric object to represent variables (the bars will be used to represent the values of the *Patience* variable along the X axis),
- Mapped the values of each variable to the levels of the aesthetic (the height of the bar along the Y axis indicates the count for each value of the *Patience* variable, by default),
- Chosen a geometric object to represent the transformed data (we used *geom_bar()* in order to draw a barchart), and
- Placed the geometric objects onto a coordinate system (the X and Y axes) using the default option.

Also, be sure to note that in *ggplot* the lines of code are connected by plus signs (" + ") rather than by a pipe (" %>% ") and that this plus sign must come at the end of a line of code rather than at the beginning of a line.

Go ahead and run these lines of code to produce a graph in the *Plots* tab in RStudio's lower right-hand pane. It will look like Figure 6.2.

Now let's use the following R code to create a bar chart displaying percentages rather than counts.

```
patience_data %>%
  ggplot(mapping = aes(x = Patience, y = ..prop.. * 100, group = 1)) +
  geom_bar()
```

Note that this code instructs the *geom_bar()* function to use the *proportion* statistical transformation rather than the default *count* transformation. The two dots on either side of *prop* (that is, "*..prop..*") instructs

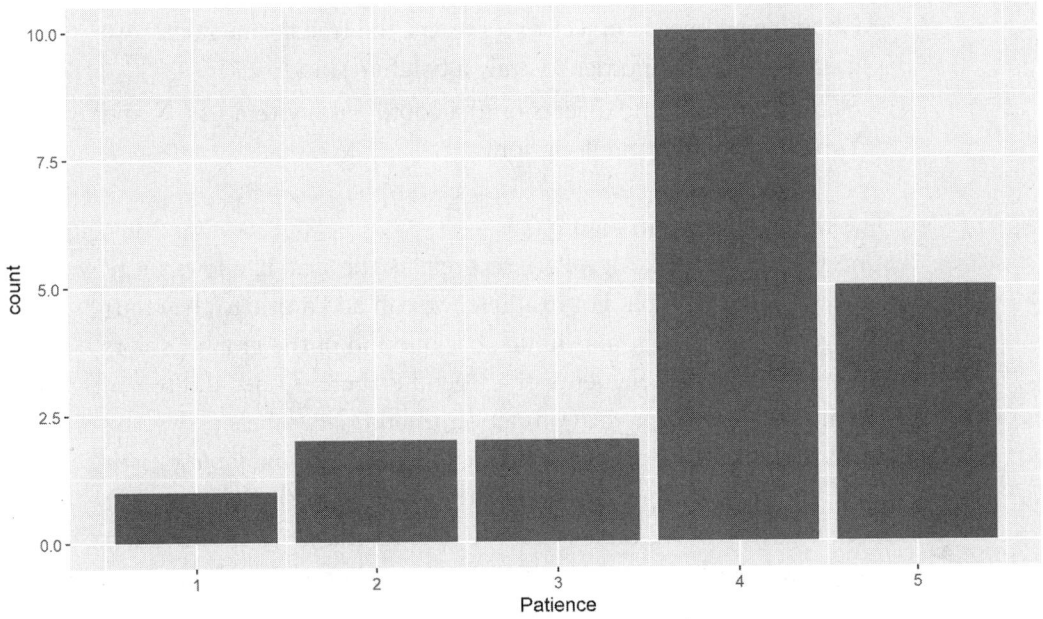

FIGURE 6.2. Default bar chart showing counts.

the *geom_bar()* function to use its internal calculation of proportions. The *group* = *1* option instructs the *geom_bar()* function to compute the proportions based on the total group (rather than based on each value of the variable on the X axis). Also, we multiply the proportion by 100 since we want to show percentages rather than proportions. Thus, in this code we have:

- Read the *patience_data* data frame,
- Called the *ggplot()* function,
- Transformed the data into the information to display (that is, the percentage of cases for each value of the variable *Patience*),
- Used aesthetic properties of the geometric object to represent variables (the bars will be used to represent the values of the *Patience* variable along the X axis, and the percentage of cases will be represented by the height of the bar along the Y axis),
- Mapped the values of each variable to the levels of the aesthetic (that is, the X and Y axes),

- Chosen a geometric object to represent the transformed data (we used *geom_bar()* in order to draw a barchart), and
- Placed the geometric objects onto a coordinate system (the X and Y axes) using the default option.

The result is shown in Figure 6.3.

One thing that makes *ggplot()* so great is the way it allows us to control elements in a graph. For example, we can add a title to the chart and change the axis labels, axis limits, background of the graph,[2] colors of the geometric figures, elements of a legend if there is one, and so on. We can also use the *geom_text()* function to add data labels above the bars. Notice that in the following code we use the *count* and *prop* statistical transformations, and we also adjust the position of the label so that it is more readable (if we omit *vjust = 0.5*, then the labels will overlap somewhat with the bars, and we can feel free to run the code without

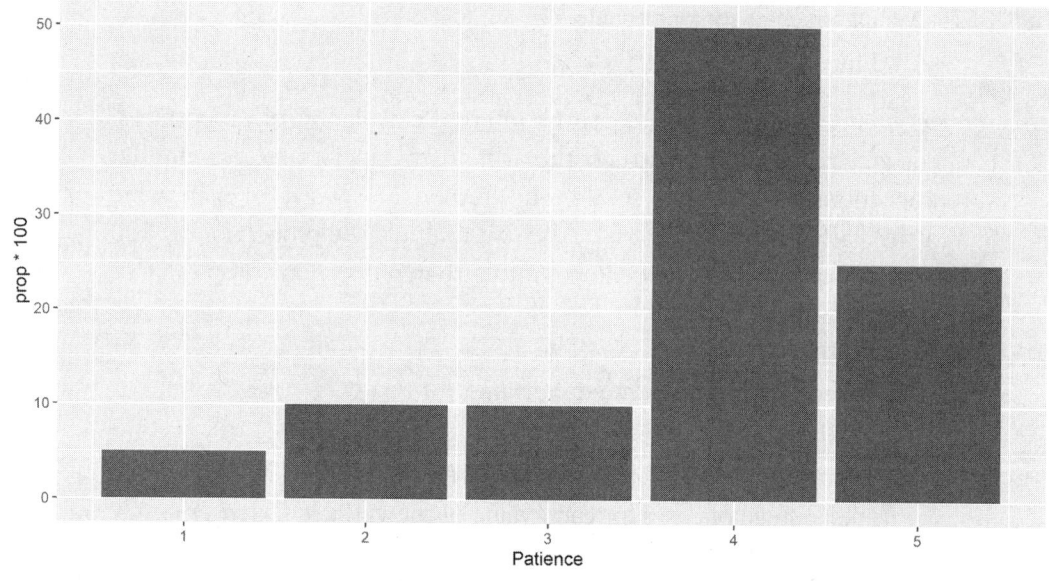

FIGURE 6.3. Default bar chart showing percentages.

_____

[2] More information about themes is available here: *https://ggplot2.tidyverse.org/reference/ggtheme.html*

that instruction to see the difference). Let's use the following code to build on the previous code and improve the graph.

```
patience_data %>%                                              # 1
  ggplot(aes(x = Patience, y = ..prop.. * 100, group = 1)) +   # 2
  geom_bar() +                                                 # 3
  ylim(0, 100) +                                               # 4
  labs(title = "Level of Patience During a Learning Task",     # 5
       x = "Patience",                                         # 6
       y = "Percentage") +                                     # 7
  geom_text(aes(label = round(..prop.. * 100, 1)),             # 8
            stat = "count", vjust = -0.5) +                    # 9
  theme_bw()                                                   # 10
```

Here are some notes to help clarify what *ggplot()* is doing in this code, referenced by line number:

- Line 1) Read the data frame,
- Line 2) Call the *ggplot()* function and map the X and Y variables,
- Line 3) Call the *geom_bar()* function,
- Line 4) Set the limits of the Y axis,
- Line 5) Add the title,
- Line 6) Label the X variable,
- Line 7) Label the Y variable,
- Lines 8 and 9) Call the *geom_text()* function, indicate that the text labels for the bars will be percentages based on the counts in each level of the variable being graphed, and adjust the vertical position of the labels to improve readability, and
- Line 10) Call the *theme_bw()* function to specify the background for the graph.

The result is shown in Figure 6.4.

Another great thing we can do with *ggplot()* is to facet the plot into small multiples, that is, to create a set of plots for levels of another variable. For example, the following R code creates two plots showing level of Patience, one for Group 1 and another for Group 2. This faceting is accomplished using the *facet_wrap()* function (or *facet_grid()* function if one is faceting by two variables rather than one); in the fourth line of code in this example we have written: *facet_wrap(~Group)*.

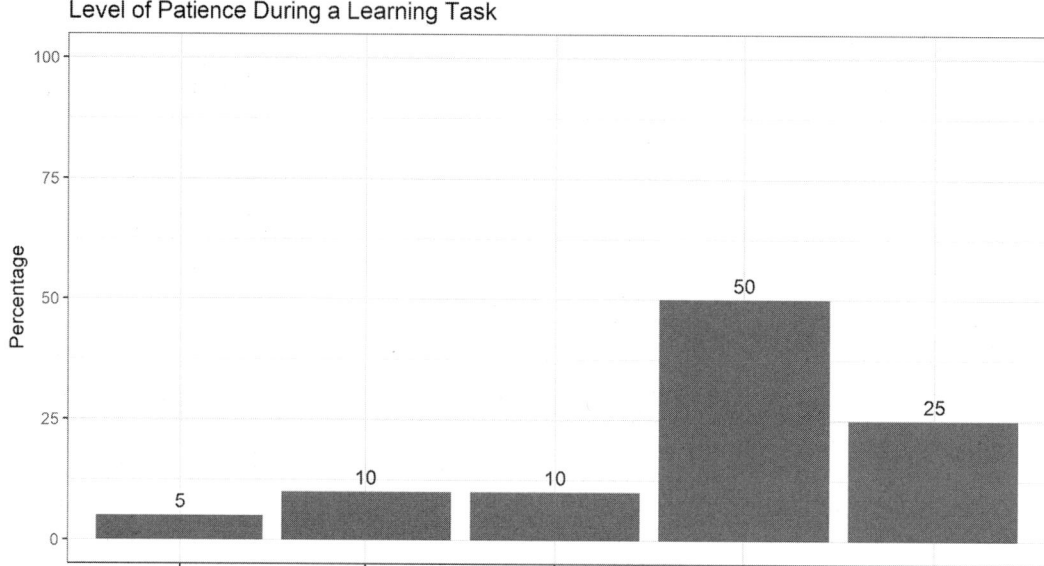

FIGURE 6.4. Formatted bar chart with data labels.

```
patience_data %>%
  ggplot(aes(x = Patience, y = ..prop.. * 100, group = 1)) +
  geom_bar() +
  facet_wrap(~Group) +
  ylim(0, 100) +
  labs(title = "Level of Patience During a Learning Task, By Group",
       x = "Patience",
       y = "Percentage") +
  geom_text(aes(label = round(..prop.. * 100, 1)),
            stat = "count", vjust = -0.5) +
  theme_bw()
```

The result is shown in Figure 6.5.

An alternative method for preparing the data for use in creating a graph is to first create a data frame with the results of the statistical transformation of interest. As an example, we could use the following R code to create Figure 6.5. First, we create the new data frame and display it to see that it has the number and percentage for each value of the variable *Patience*. We then draw the graph, using *stat* = *"identity"* to use the data as they are rather than transforming them (since they were already transformed when the new data frame was created). Similarly, we can use this approach (that is, *stat* = *"identity"*) if we only have the results that we want to graph, which may occur if someone provides you with just the results and you need to graph them.

```
patience_data2 %>%
  ggplot(aes(x = Patience, y = Percentage)) +
  geom_bar(stat = "identity") +
  #  geom_bar(stat = "identity", color = "blue", fill = "red") +
  ylim(0, 100) +
  labs(title = "Level of Patience While Learning a Task",
       x = "Patience",
       y = "Percentage") +
  geom_text(label = patience_data2$Percentage, vjust = -0.5) +
  theme_bw()
```

In addition, we have tremendous control over the coloring of the bars. For example, if in the code above we comment out the second line and uncomment the third line, we will create bars that have a blue

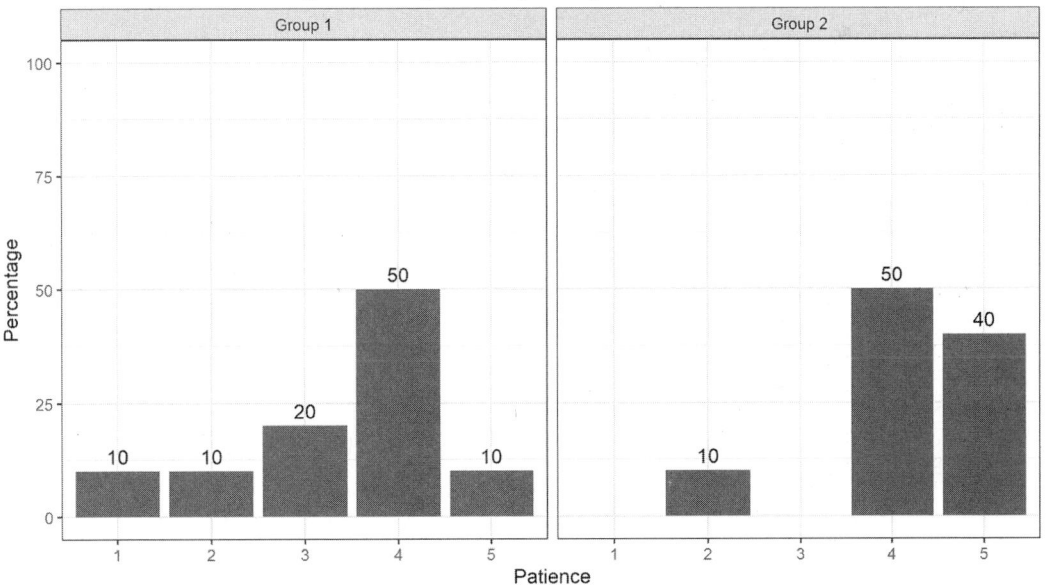

FIGURE 6.5. Faceted bar chart.

outline and red interior. Information about *ggplot2* aesthetic specifications can be found at *https://ggplot2.tidyverse.org/articles/ggplot2-specs.html*.

Let's take one more look at some ways we can build elements of a graph. Suppose, for example, that we ask 50 people to pick their favorite food from a list of five foods that we show to them. We then want to draw a bar chart to show the result, sorted in order of preference, with the bar for the favorite food highlighted. The following code accomplishes this task.

```
# Create variables
foods  <- factor(c("Food 1", "Food 2", "Food 3", "Food 4", "Food 5"))
people <- c(7, 10, 18, 12, 3)
# Create data frame
favorites <- data.frame(foods, people)
# Display data frame
favorites
# Draw graph
favorites %>%                                          # 1
  mutate(highlight = ifelse(foods == "Food 3",         # 2
                       "Highlighted", "Normal")) %>%   # 3
  ggplot(mapping = aes(x = reorder(foods, people),     # 4
                  y = people,                          # 5
                  fill = highlight)) +                 # 6
  geom_bar(stat = "identity", width = .5) +            # 7
  scale_fill_grey() +                                  # 8
  geom_text(label = favorites$people, hjust = -0.5) +  # 9
  ylim(0, 20) +                                        # 10
  labs(title = "Favorite Foods",                       # 11
       x = "Foods",                                    # 12
       y = "Number of People") +                       # 13
  theme_bw() +                                         # 14
  theme(legend.position = "none") +                    # 15
  coord_flip()                                         # 16
```

Here are some notes to help clarify what *ggplot()* is doing in this code, referenced by line number:

- Line 1) Read the data frame.
- Lines 2 and 3) Use the *mutate()* function to create a variable to indicate which value of X to highlight, by using the *ifelse()* function, which tests a condition, indicates what to do if the condition is true and what to do if the condition is not true. In our lines of code, we first test whether the variable *foods* has the value of *Food*

3. If it does, it should be highlighted, and if not, it should not be highlighted.

- Lines 4 through 6) Call *ggplot()* and map the X variable ordered by the number of people for each value of the variable, the Y variable, and the fill (that is, which bar to highlight).
- Line 7) Call the *geom_bar()* function, specify the *stat*, and set the width of the bars.
- Line 8) Make the highlighted bar black and the others gray.
- Line 9) Add the data label and adjust its position.
- Line 10) Set the limits of the Y axis.
- Lines 11–13) Add the title and the X and Y axis labels.
- Line 14) Choose the background.
- Line 15) Remove the legend (we can create the graph without this line of code so that the legend appears, which will help clarify why it is not necessary in this example).
- Line 16) Flip the graph so that the bars are horizontal rather than vertical.

The resulting graph is shown in Figure 6.6.

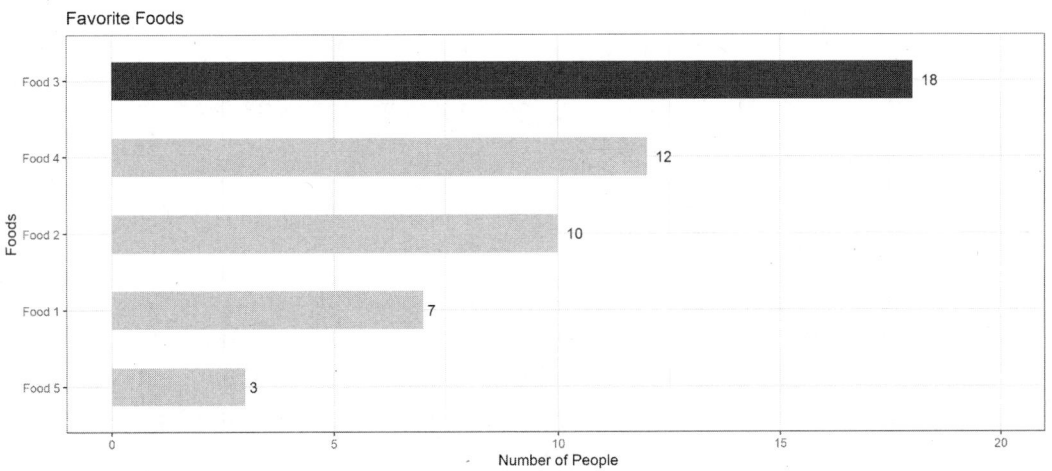

FIGURE 6.6. Highlighting a bar in a bar chart.

Boxplot

In this section we use the *ggplot()* function to draw boxplots. A boxplot illustrates the distribution of a set of values. It consists of a box that encompasses the interquartile range (IQR), that is, the distance from the 25th to 75th percentile of the distribution. The median is drawn in the middle of the box. A whisker extends from each end of the box to the farthest point that is not an outlier in the distribution. Observations that are more than 1.5 times the IQR from either end of the box are considered outliers and are plotted individually. We can use the following R code to obtain descriptive statistics and to draw boxplots for the report card data that we used in Chapter 4 to conduct an independent sample *t*-test.

```
#Create the data frame
timing <- c("Weekly", "Weekly", "Weekly", "Weekly", "Weekly",
            "Weekly", "Weekly", "Weekly", "Weekly", "Weekly",
            "Nine-week", "Nine-week", "Nine-week", "Nine-week",
            "Nine-week", "Nine-week", "Nine-week", "Nine-week",
            "Nine-week", "Nine-week")
motivation <- c(75, 68, 87, 80, 65, 80, 82, 75 ,75 ,55,
                69, 68, 69, 72, 69, 68, 64, 68, 67, 68)
timing <- factor(timing)
report_card <- data.frame(timing, motivation)

# Draw the box plot
report_card %>%
  ggplot(aes(x = timing, y = motivation)) +
  geom_boxplot() +
  ylim(50, 100) +
  labs(title = "Level of Motivation for Groups Receiving
Report Cards at Different Intervals",
       x = "Frequency of Report Cards",
       y = "Motivation") +
  theme_gray()
```

This code reads the data frame, calls the *ggplot()* function, maps the variable *timing* to the X axis and the variable *motivation* to the Y axis, calls the *geom_boxplot()* function, titles the graph, labels the X and Y axes, and calls the *theme_gray()* function to set the background for the graph. The result is shown in Figure 6.7.

As another example, we can use the following R code to obtain summary statistics and to draw bar charts for the blood pressure data that we used in Chapter 4 to conduct a dependent sample *t*-test.

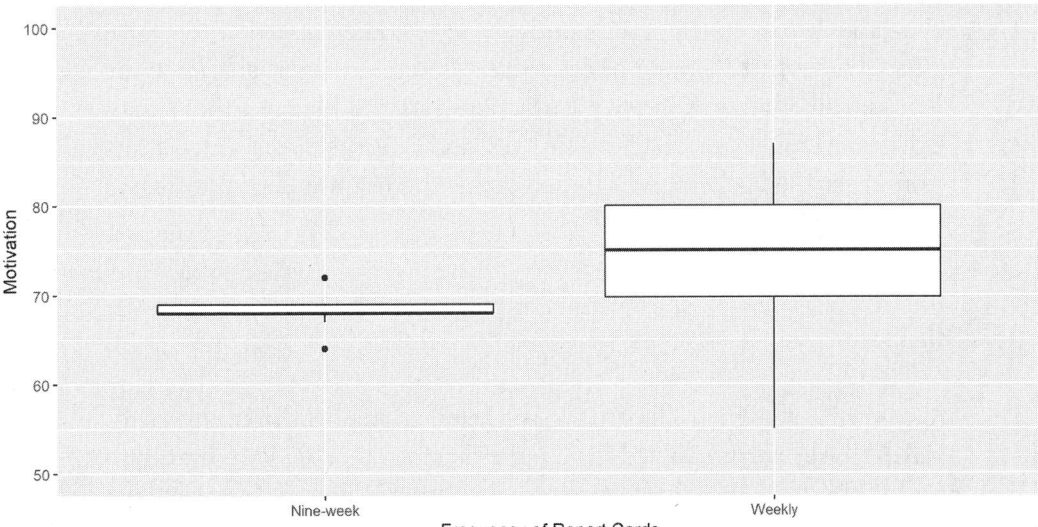

FIGURE 6.7. Boxplot for report card data.

```
# Create the data frame
patient <- c(1, 2, 3, 4, 5, 6, 7, 8, 9, 10)
time <- c("Before", "Before", "Before", "Before", "Before", "Before",
"Before", "Before", "Before", "Before",
          "After", "After","After","After","After", "After",
"After","After","After","After")
bp <- c(120, 117, 119, 130, 121, 105, 128, 114, 109, 120,
        135, 118, 131, 128, 121, 115, 124, 111, 117, 120)
time <- factor(time)
bp_study <- data.frame(patient, time, bp)
# Get summary statistics
bp_study %>%
  group_by(time) %>%
  get_summary_stats(bp)
# Draw the boxplot
bp_study %>%
  ggplot(aes(x = time, aes(x = factor(time, level = c('Before', 'After')),
            y = bp)) +
  geom_boxplot() +
  ylim(90, 140) +
  labs(title = "Blood Pressure at Times: Before and After",
      x = "Time of Measurement",
      y = "Blood Pressure") +
  theme_gray()
```

This code reads the data frame, calls the *ggplot()* function, maps the variable *time* to the X axis (with the levels ordered so that the value *Before* comes first followed by the value *After*) and the variable *bp* to the Y axis, calls the *geom_boxplot()* function, sets the limits of the Y axis, titles the graph, labels the X and Y axes, and calls the *theme_gray()* function to set the background for the graph. The result is shown in Figure 6.8.

Line Graph

We now draw a graph illustrating the interaction effect from the factorial ANOVA we conducted in Chapter 5. The following R code accomplishes this task. We first obtain the summary statistics and display them in the Console in order to have them close by for reference, and then we draw the graph. By recalling that we can read the pipe (" %>% ") as " . . . then . . . , " we can read the following lines of code as (1) reference the data frame, (2) group the data by the two variables of interest, (3) get

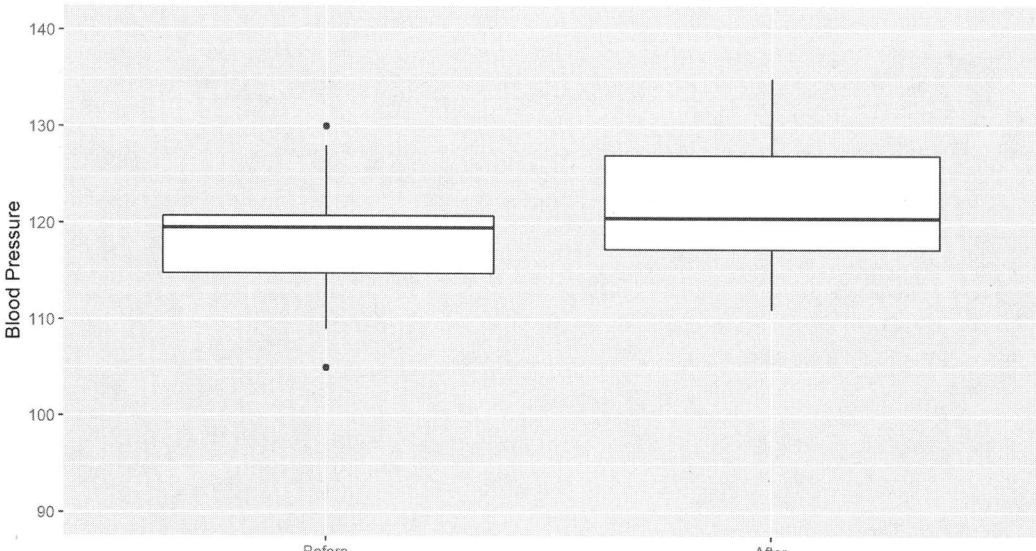

FIGURE 6.8. Boxplot for blood pressure data.

the summary statistics by group, and (4) pass those summary statistics to *ggplot()* for use in drawing the graph.

```
# Create data frame
technology <- factor(rep(c("Computer", "Calculator"), times = c(20, 20)))
age_group <- factor(rep(c("30 or younger", "Over 30", "30 or younger", "Over 30"),
                        times = c(10, 10, 10, 10)))
score <- c(68, 67, 66, 73, 75, 69, 70, 71, 73, 74,
           79, 80, 76, 71, 72, 75, 75, 72, 71, 74,
           73, 73, 77, 77, 75, 77, 78, 69, 70, 71,
           70, 74, 75, 72, 72, 69, 73, 75, 76, 72)
tech_age   <- data.frame(technology, age_group, score)

# Descriptive statistics for each combination of technology type and age group
tech_age %>%
  group_by(technology, age_group) %>%
  get_summary_stats(show = c("n", "min", "max", "median", "mean",
                             "sd", "se", "ci"))

# Graph showing interaction
tech_age %>%
  group_by(technology, age_group) %>%
  get_summary_stats(score) %>%
  ggplot(aes(x = factor(technology, level = c('Computer', 'Calculator')),
             y = mean, group = age_group, linetype = age_group)) +
  geom_point() +
  geom_line() +
  ylim(70, 75) +
  labs(title = "Score by Techology Use and Age Group",
       x = "Technology", y = "Mean Score",
       linetype = "Age Group") +
  theme_classic()
```

The *ggplot()* function in the code above proceeds as follows: (1) Define the aesthetic properties of the object that will represent variables (the variable *technology* will be on the X axis with the levels ordered so that the value *Computer* comes first followed by the value *Calculator*), and the group means will be shown on the Y axis connected by different types of lines (one will be solid and one will be dotted) for the two groups rather than having lines of only one type; (2) use the *geom_point()* function to add a point for each of the four means; (3) use the *geom_line()* function to add a line between the means of each age group; (4) set the limits of the Y axis; (5) add labels to the graph; and (6) call the *theme_classic()* function to set the background for the graph. The result is shown in Figure 6.9.

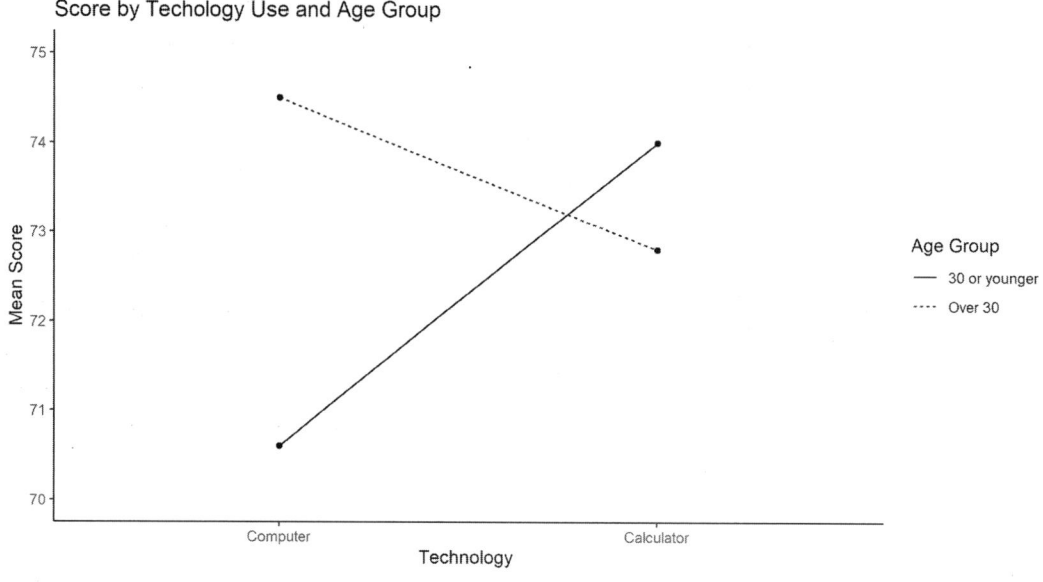

FIGURE 6.9. Line graph showing ANOVA interaction effect.

As another example, let's draw a graph illustrating results from the repeated measures ANOVA we conducted in Chapter 5. The following R code, very similar to what we used just above, accomplishes this task. Notice that we are using the data frame that is in long format rather than the original data frame in wide format, as that is what *ggplot()* needs. Again, we first obtain the summary statistics and display them in the Console in order to have them close by for reference, and then we draw the graph. We can read the following lines of code as (1) reference the data frame, (2) group the data by the two variables of interest, (3) get the summary statistics by group, and (4) pass those summary statistics to *ggplot()* for use in drawing the graph.

```
# Create the data frame
participant <- rep(1:10)
time1 <- c(3, 1, 1, 4, 1, 1, 3, 4, 1, 1)
time2 <- c(4, 3, 6, 3, 7, 5, 5, 6, 7, 4)
time3 <- c(6, 10, 9, 10, 8, 9, 9, 9, 7, 10)
interest <- data.frame(participant, time1, time2, time3)

# Reformat the data
interest_long <- interest %>%
```

```
  pivot_longer(c(time1, time2, time3),
             names_to = "time", values_to = "interest")

# View the data
interest
interest_long# Descriptive statistics from the reformatted data frame
interest_long %>%
  group_by(time) %>%
  get_summary_stats(interest,
                    show = c("n", "min", "max", "median", "mean",
                             "sd", "se", "ci"))

# Graph the repeated measures ANOVA
interest_long %>%
  group_by(time) %>%
  get_summary_stats(interest) %>%
  ggplot(aes(x =     time,
             y =     mean,
             group = 1)) +
  geom_point() +
  geom_line(stat = "identity") +
  geom_errorbar(aes(ymin = (mean - se ), ymax = (mean + se )), width = .1) +
  ylim(0, 10) +
  labs(title = "Level of Interest",
       x = "Time", y = "Mean +/- One Standard Error") +
  theme_classic()
```

The *ggplot()* function in the above code proceeds as follows: (1) define the aesthetic properties of the object that will represent variables (the variable *time* will be displayed on the X axis, the *mean* of each group will be displayed on the Y axis, and the *group* =1 instruction causes the line to be drawn that connects the points representing the group means); (2) call the *geom_point()* function to add a point for each of the three means; (3) call the *geom_line()* function to add a line between the means of each group; (4) call the *geom_errobar()* function to add an error bar around each mean and set its width, (5) set the limits of the Y axis; (6) add labels to the graph; and (7) select the theme for the background of the graph. The result is shown in Figure 6.10.

Scatterplot

In this section we will draw scatterplots that are commonly used in regression analyses. We will first create a scatterplot for the correlation

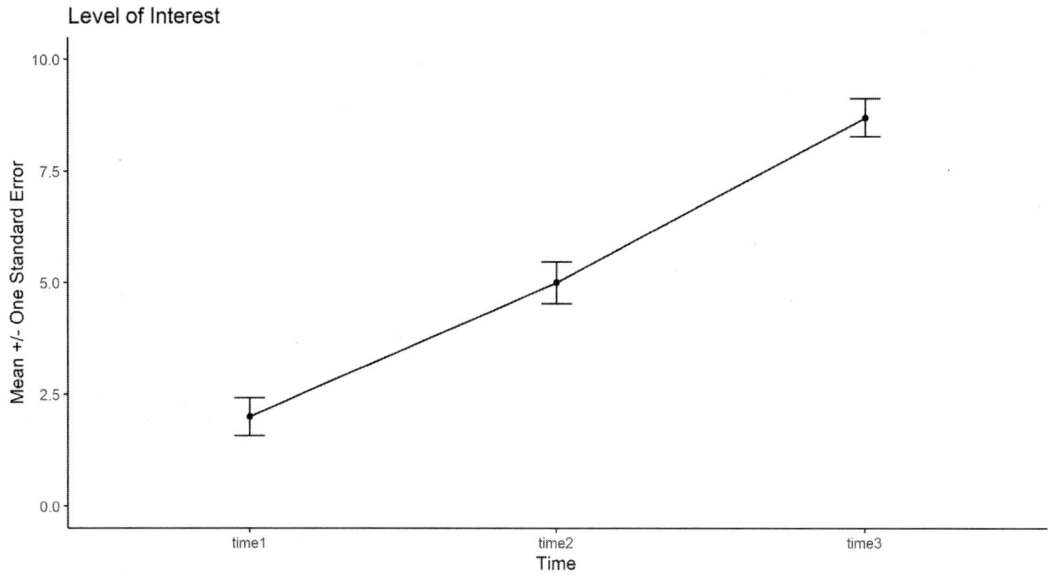

FIGURE 6.10. Line graph showing results from a repeated-measures ANOVA.

between absences from class and score on a final exam that we used in Chapter 5. The following R code accomplishes this task.

```
# Create the data frame
absences <- c(1, 2, 4, 5, 6, 4, 6, 7, 2, 7,
              7, 9, 11, 2, 1, 12, 6, 7, 2,3)
score <- c(100, 95, 90, 90, 80, 85, 82, 80, 97, 77,
           70, 90, 55, 94, 90, 70, 80, 80, 93, 88)
go_to_class <- data.frame(absences, score)

# Look at the data frame
go_to_class

# Draw the graph
go_to_class %>%
  ggplot(aes(x = score, y =  absences)) +
  geom_point() +
  xlim(50, 100) +
  ylim(0, 15) +
  geom_smooth(method = "lm", se = FALSE, color = "black") +
  labs(title = "Scatterplot of Absences and Final Exam Score",
       x = "Score", y = "Absences") +
  theme_classic()
```

The *ggplot()* function in the code above proceeds as follows: (1) define the aesthetic properties of the object that will represent variables (the variable *score* will be displayed on the X axis, and the variable *absences* will be displayed on the Y axis), (2) call the *geom_point()* function to add a point for each observation; (3) set the limits of the X and Y axes; (4) call the *geom_smooth()* function to add a regression line (you can also display the 95% confidence interval around the line if you remove *se = FALSE* in the *geom_smooth()* function); (5) add labels to the graph; and (6) call the *theme_classic()* function to select the theme for the background of the graph. The result is shown in Figure 6.11.

Regression Diagnostics

One way to obtain a variety of graphs for regression diagnostics is to use the *ggResidpanel* package. For example, the default charts produced by the *resid_panel()* function include: residual plot (residuals on the Y axis

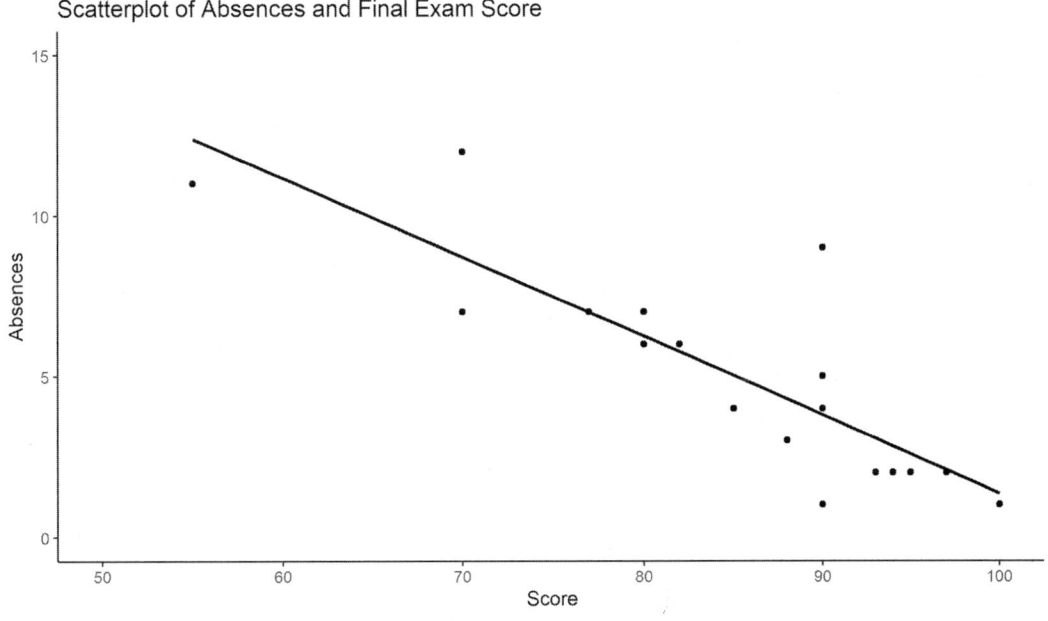

FIGURE 6.11. Scatterplot with regression line.

and predicted values on the X axis), Q-Q plot (normal quantile plot of the residuals), index plot (residuals on the Y axis and observation number associated with the residual on the X axis), and histogram (histogram of the residuals with overlaid density curve with mean equal to zero and standard deviation equal to the standard deviation of the residuals). The following R code accomplishes this task for the regression of *score on a final exam* on *absences*, which we used in Chapter 5 and again in Figure 6.11 above.

```
# Load ggResdpanel package
library(ggResidpanel)

# Create default plots from model
resid_panel(lm(score ~ absences, go_to_class))

# Create object from model and then create default plots using the model
#    (same result as previous line)
go_to_class.model <- lm(score ~ absences, go_to_class)
resid_panel(go_to_class.model)

# Show all plots from resid_panel() function
resid_panel(go_to_class.model, plots = "all")
```

The result (default plots) is shown in Figure 6.12.

Saving a Chart

We can save a chart using the *ggsave()* function. This function saves the most recent chart displayed to a file with the filename provided. A variety of formats are available, including .png, .jpeg, .pdf, and others. The file is saved to the current working directory unless a pathname to another directory is specified. For example, the following R code saves the regression diagnostics charts we created in the previous section to a file in the current directory called *go_to_class_panel.png*.

```
# Create and save regression panel default plots to current working directory
resid_panel(lm(score ~ absences, go_to_class))
ggsave("go_to_class_panel.png")
```

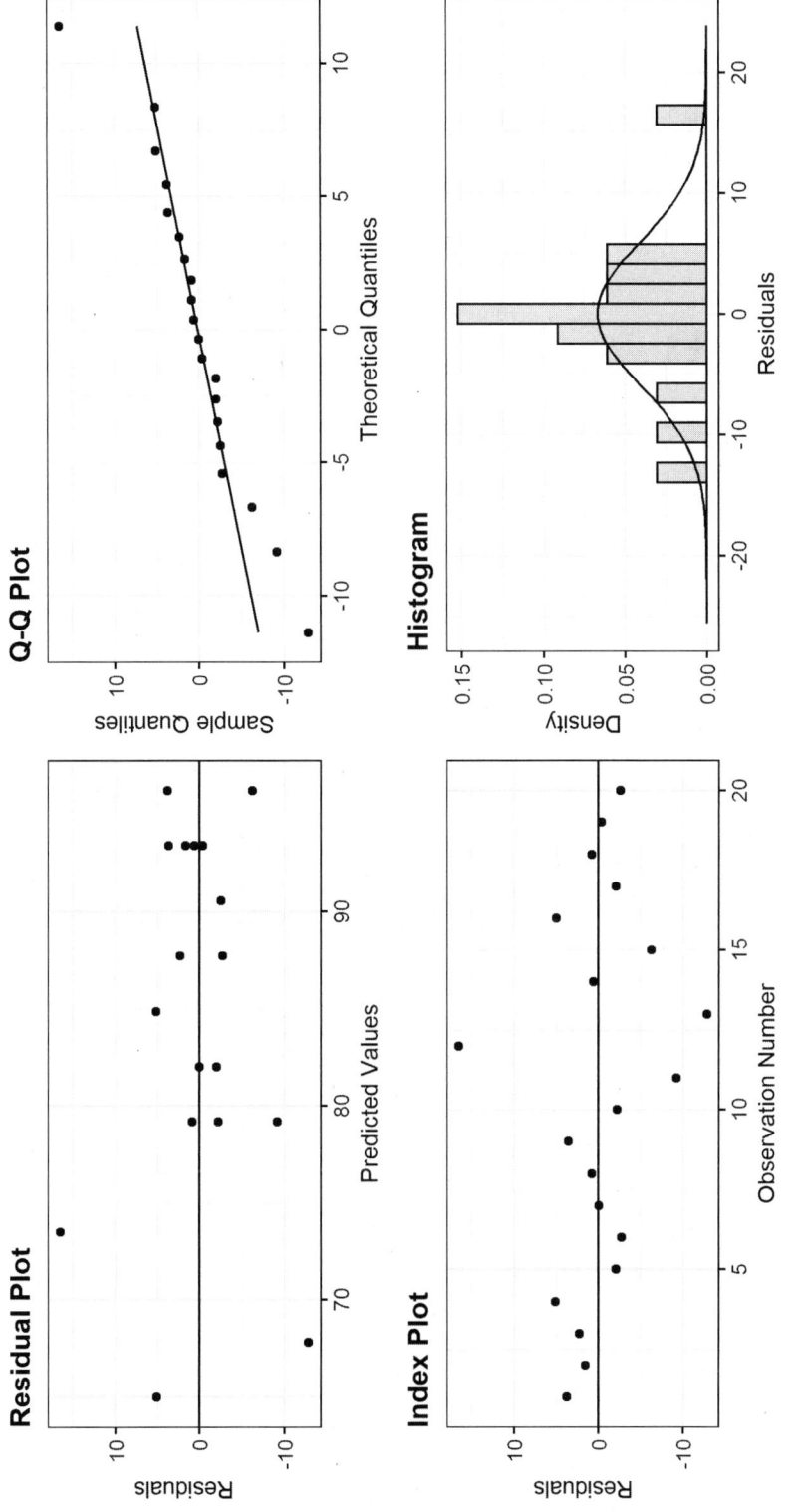

FIGURE 6.12. Regression diagnostic plots.

▲ KEY TAKEAWAYS

▲ By understanding the layered grammar of graphics we can think about how to go about creating any graph we can imagine.

▲ The *ggplot2* package has remarkable, extensive capabilities for creating graphs.

▲ The *ggplot()* function is designed to work with tidy data.

EXERCISES

1. Re-create the graph shown in Figure 6.6, but show the bars in color rather than in black and gray, by replacing the code

    ```
    scale_fill_grey() + # 8
    ```

    with the code

    ```
    scale_fill_manual(values = c("Highlighted" = "blue2",
    "Normal" = "green3")) +
    ```

2. Use the *colors()* function to review the colors already available in R, select two of your choice, and re-create the graph in the exercise above using those colors rather than the colors *blue2* and *green3*.

3. Using the data in the section on Oneway ANOVA in Chapter 4 (effect of three types of instruction on math achievement), draw a boxplot to show the distribution of grades for each of the three instructional methods.

4. Use the *ggplot()* function to create a scatterplot with a regression line from the data in Chapter 5, Exercise 1.

R Markdown

In addition to performing data analysis tasks, R can output the results of analyses to various formats (for example, a Word document, HTML, a PowerPoint presentation) along with accompanying text. This capability eases report writing and facilitates research reproducibility. As defined by Bollen et al. (2015, pp. 3–4), reproducibility

> refers to the ability of a researcher to duplicate the results of a prior study using the same materials and procedures as were used by the original investigator. So in an attempt to reproduce a published statistical analysis, a second researcher might use the same raw data to build the same analysis files and implement the same statistical analysis to determine whether they yield the same results. . . . Reproducibility is a minimum necessary condition for a finding to be believable and informative.

The National Academies of Sciences, Engineering, and Medicine (2019) has considered reproducibility and replicability in detail. They define these terms as follows (pp. 6–7):

Reproducibility is obtaining consistent results using the same input data; computational steps, methods, and code; and conditions of analysis. This definition is synonymous with "computational reproducibility," and the terms are used interchangeably in this report.

Replicability is obtaining consistent results across studies aimed at answering the same scientific question, each of which has obtained its own data. Two studies may be considered to have replicated if they obtain consistent results given the level of uncertainty inherent in the system under study.

Generalizability, another term frequently used in science, refers to the extent that results of a study apply in other contexts or populations that differ from the original one.[1] A single scientific study may include elements or any combination of these concepts. In short, reproducibility involves the *original* data and code; replicability involves *new* data collection to test for consistency with previous results of a similar study.

In this chapter we will begin an exploration of the world of R Markdown to integrate data analysis and reporting. Not only is R Markdown useful in promoting research reproducibility, it also makes it easier (and less error-prone) to update a report when incorporating new data, rerunning analyses, or making other changes that affect the analyses or reporting.

Markdown Template

We begin by creating a new Markdown file from the pull-down menu: **File → New File → R Markdown . . .** This opens the New R Markdown dialog box shown in Figure 7.1. In this dialog box, we have options to create a document (in HTML, PDF, and Word formats), presentation (in HTML, PDF, and PowerPoint formats), and an interactive document or presentation using Shiny[2], or we can use some other template (we can even create our own reusable template).

Let's choose to create a Word document. As noted in the dialog box, we can later change to another format. This opens the document

---

[1] The same definition of generalizability as used by NSF (Bollen et al., 2015).

[2] To learn more about Shiny, visit: *https://shiny.rstudio.com.*

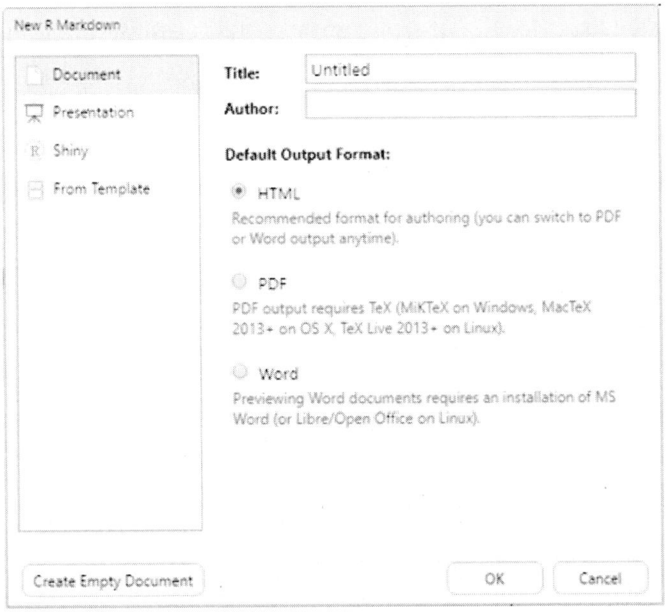

FIGURE 7.1. New R Markdown dialog box.

template (clicking the Create *Empty Document* button will open a blank file rather than a template).

Let's examine this file closely. Lines 1 through 4 contain the YAML (YAML Ain't Markup Language) header that presents options for how the document will be rendered. The YAML code appears between two lines of three hyphens (" --- "). Next are alternating chunks of white and gray areas. The white areas include text and text formatting commands. The gray areas contain R code.

Each chunk of R code begins with " ``` {r} " and ends with " ``` " (the backticks are located on the same keyboard key as the tilde). The chunks of R code can be named for convenience (that is, *setup*). They can also contain options; for example, *echo = FALSE* shows the results in the output document but does not show the code in the output document, and *include = FALSE* keeps both the code and the results from being displayed in the output document. The first chunk of R code includes setup options that apply to the entire document unless different options are specified for a later chunk of code. Each chunk of text contains text, and associated formatting, that will appear in the output document. For example, the two hashmarks (" ## ") at the beginning of a line cause that line to appear in the output document as a level two header.

We can run individual chunks of R code by placing the cursor on the desired part(s) in the code and running it in the usual way (for example, by pressing Ctrl+Enter). We can also set chunk options and run chunks of code, using the icons at the upper right-hand corner of a code chunk. We can run the entire file, rendering the output document, by clicking the **Knit** button (the one with the ball of yarn and needles) just above the Markdown script, or from the pull-down menu from **File →
Knit Document** or with **Cntrl + Shift + K**.

By looking at the file, we can anticipate what the output document will include: the title *Untitled*, a level two header that says *R Markdown* followed by some text, summary statistics for the two variables in the *cars* data frame (which is already available as part of Base R), another level two header followed by text, a graph plotting the two variables in the *pressure* dataframe, and then some final text. Go ahead and **Knit** the document, watch the progress in the Console, and then compare the document that is produced to the Markdown file that produced it.

Working in Markdown

Now let's create our own Markdown document. We will use the example from Terrell (2021) that we used for the chi-square analysis in Chapter 4.

Open Markdown Template, Enter First Lines of Code, and Knit

Open a new Word document template, either by clicking the *Create Empty Document* button in the bottom left corner of the dialog box or by opening the template without clicking that button and deleting the code it contains. We will enter our code part by part, knitting the file along the way to see how it develops and how we can control the output. Along the way, be aware that on occasion you may need to close an output file, or even exit and re-launch RStudio (remember to save your work first), just to reset.

Let's begin with the following lines of code. The first four lines are the YAML header, stating the title and author, and choosing to output a Word document. The next set of lines (between the two sets of three backticks (" ``` ") contains the first chunk of R code. The first line of this chunk begins with a curly brace, is followed by the letter "r," an optional name for the chunk (here it is *setup*), a comma, and the *include = FALSE* instruction to keep the chunk from being included in the output. Next comes an overall setting for the file, which is *echo = FALSE*, so that our default setting is to not include the R code in the output. We then load the packages we will use in this program (it is good to load all the packages we need at the beginning of the file). In the line that reads *# Load Packages*, the " # " at the beginning of the line indicates that it is a comment since it is inside a chunk of R code.

After the three backticks that end the R code chunk (in gray), we are in the text area (in white). In the line that reads *## Introduction*, the " ## " at the beginning of the line instructs R Markdown that this is a level two header. We then have a line of text, followed by an indented block indicated by the " > " at the beginning of the text.

```
---
title: "Graduation Status by Learning Style"
author: "Your Name Here"
output: word_document
---

```{r setup, include=FALSE}
knitr::opts_chunk$set(echo = FALSE)

# Load packages
library(tidyverse)
library(rstatix)
library(flextable)

```


Introduction

In this document we look at an example from Terrell (2021):

> Throughout the world, more and more colleges and universities
are introducing distance learning programs... Some people are
critical of these programs because they feel they may not equally
support all learning styles and therefore may lead to failure in
such a learning environment... By analyzing the interaction of
learning style and attrition, we will be able to determine if the
concerns about distance education are warranted. (p.327)
```

Go ahead and knit this file. The first time it is knitted we are prompted for a name for the file, since it gets saved at this point. Knitting progress is displayed in the Console. Once done, a Word document is opened, and you will see the title, author, level two header, and text that we wrote.

Create and Look at a Data Frame

Let's now add the next R code chunk. The first line begins the chunk, with three backticks, an open curly brace, the letter "r," and an optional name for the chunk. We then have groups of lines that create the dataframe and a second dataframe in long format, look at the first and last few lines of the data frame (commented out), create a third data frame with summary counts and percentages, and create an object that contains the results of the chi-square test. The code chunk ends with another set of three backticks.

```
```{r dataframe}

# Create data frame
dist_learn <- as.table(
  rbind(c(9, 16, 12, 10), c(5, 12, 6, 10)))

dimnames(dist_learn) <- list(
  Status = c("Graduate", "Non-graduate"),
  Learning_style = c("Accommodator", "Assimilator", "Diverger",
                     "Converger"))

# Convert counts to cases
dist_learn_long <- counts_to_cases(dist_learn)

# Look at data
#dist_learn_long %>%
#  slice(1:5, 76:80)

# Get counts to use in division later
summarized <- dist_learn_long %>%
  group_by(Status) %>%
  summarize(n = n()) %>%
  mutate(Percent = prop.table(n)) %>%
  mutate(Percent = Percent * 100) %>%
  mutate(Percent = round(Percent, 1))

# Conduct chi_square test
csq <- chisq.test(dist_learn_long$Status, dist_learn_long$Learning_style)

```
```

We can run the R code from within the R Markdown document by placing our cursor on the part of interest and then running it as usual. The result appears just below the code chunk (you may need to scroll down to see it). This is good to do, as once the file gets longer it is easier to test the code that way (and debug if necessary) than by knitting (rendering) the document. Go ahead and test the code, and once it is working, knit the file again. Since this code chunk did not produce anything that is displayed, none appears in the output document. We do see a message, but we know from Chapter 4 that in this instance the message is not important for us. Therefore, we can edit the first line of this code chunk to read:

```
```{r dataframe, message = FALSE}
```

Create the Crosstabulation Table

Let's now add the following lines of code. First, we have another level two header, followed by a line of text. Then we have an R code chunk (again, beginning and ending with three backticks). This chunk contains a comment, and then it uses the *proc_freq()* function from the *rstatix* package to create a *flextable* that displays a table in our Word document. The first line in the *proc_freq()* function names the variables to include in the table and provides a title for the table, the next two lines suppress the column and cell percentages, the two lines after that relabel a variable and suppress a column header, and the final line fits the table on the page.

```
## Crosstabulation table

Next, we create the crosstabulation table.

```{r crosstab, echo = FALSE}
# Create the crosstabulation table
dist_learn_long %>%
  proc_freq("Learning_style", "Status", "Status by Learning Style",
          include.column_percent = FALSE,
          include.table_percent = FALSE) %>%
  set_header_labels(Learning_style = "Learning Style",
              label = "") %>%
  autofit()
```
```
```

Go ahead and knit the document again, and notice that the output now includes the *flextable*. Now is a good time to explore what this code is doing by altering it, re-knitting, and comparing the output to what it was before. I suggest trying these things one at a time and re-knitting with each change before returning to the original:

- Set *echo* to TRUE, delete "*Status by Learning Style*,"
- Set *include.column_percent* to TRUE,
- Sset *include.table_percent* to TRUE,
- Remove the *set_header_labels(...)* and note that this causes two differences, and
- Remove *autofit()* and the pipe (" %>% ") that precedes it.

This sort of practice is a good way to get familiar with writing code. It is especially beneficial if you work on predicting how the change will affect the result and then checking the accuracy of your prediction. If your prediction was not correct, think about why and how you would predict differently next time. This kind of exercise will help you in the future, when you want to accomplish something with your R code and you are figuring out the puzzle of how to do it.

Conduct a Chi-Square Test and Embed Results within Text

Now let's add some more code, all of which is in the R Markdown text area. The first line instructs R Markdown to begin a new output page (using the *\newpage* instruction). The next line is another level two header, which is followed by a line of text. We then use the asterisk at the beginning of the line to instruct R Markdown to create a bullet point. This bullet point includes embedded R code, which begins with a backtick followed by the letter "r" and ends with another backtick ('r . . .'). This bullet point uses the *nrow()* function to include the number of cases in the bullet point, so that we expect that in the output it will read "The results are based on the 80 cases in our data frame." One great thing about this is that if the data frame gets changed (for example, if more cases are added to it), this bullet point will automatically be updated the next time the file is knit. We then have two bullet points that draw results from our summarized data frame. The last bullet point uses information from the object named *csq*, which we created to contain the results of the chi-square analysis. We use the Base R naming convention *object$variable* to refer to the items that we want. You may find it helpful to use the *view()* function to display the *csq* object so that you can take a look at it by entering and running *view(csq)* inside one of the R code chunks. Thus, this bullet point includes:

- The degrees of freedom *csq$parameter*,
- The number of cases *nrow(dist_learn_long)* (note that the asterisk on each side of the "N" in the following text input causes the "N" to be italicized),
- The chi-square statistic rounded to three decimal places *round(csq$statistic, 3)*, and
- The probability associated with the chi-square statistic rounded to two decimal places *round(csq$p.value, 2)* (note that the asterisk on each side of the "p" in the following text input causes the "p" to be italicized).

Following the bullet points are two lines that illustrate how to include comments within the text area, which is done by using the format " <!-- ... text ... --> " As noted in the last line, to indicate that R code embedded within text should be considered a comment, we need to include both the " <!-- ... --> " for the text and the " # " for the R code.

```
\newpage

## Embed Results Into Text

As we can see from this table:

* The results are based on the `r nrow(dist_learn_long)` cases in
our data frame.

* The overall percentage who graduated was: `r summarized %>%
     filter(Status == "Graduate") %>%
     select(Percent)`.

* The overall percentage who graduated was: `r summarized %>%
     filter(Status == "Non-graduate") %>%
     select(Percent)`.
```

```
* The percentage who graduated was not different among the
different learning styles. Pearson's chi-square statistic
(`r csq$parameter`, *N* = `r nrow(dist_learn_long)`) =
`r round(csq$statistic, 3)`, *p* = `r round(csq$p.value, 2)`.

<!--    This is a comment in the RMarkdown text -->

<!-- To comment out a line with embedded R code, both the line and
        the R code need to be commented out, for example: -->
<!--    Some text here `r #some embedded R code here` then some
more text here. -->
```

Go ahead and knit the file again and study the output document side by side with the code that produced it. If necessary, debug the R Markdown file as needed.

Visualize the Results

Once the file is running correctly, let's add our last lines of code. We first have another level two header, which is followed by a line of text. We then have a new R code chunk, which uses the *ggplot()* function to create a graph. We next create a bar chart with *learning style* on the X axis and the *percent graduated* on the Y axis, set the limits of the Y axis, add a main label and labels for the two axes as well as data labels above the bars, and set the look of the background.

```
## Visualize the Results

These results are illustrated in the following graph.

```{r, graph, echo = FALSE}

# Create graph
ggplot(dist_learn_long,
       aes(x = Learning_style, y = ..prop.. * 100, group = 1)) +
  geom_bar() +
  ylim(0, 100) +
  labs(title = "Status by Learning Style",
       x = "Learning Style",
       y = "Percent Graduated") +
  geom_text(aes(label = round(..prop.. * 100, 0)),
            stat = "count", vjust = -0.5) +
  theme_bw()

```
```

Go ahead and again run the R code from within the R Markdown file. Once it is working, knit the file and examine the output file side by side with the code that produced it.

Before we end this chapter, let's look at one other output format, a PowerPoint presentation. Open a new R Markdown file from the pull-down menus (**File → New File → R Markdown . . .**) and in the **New R Markdown** dialog box select **Presentation** and **PowerPoint** (see Figure 7.2).

By now you are familiar enough with R Markdown that you can understand what is in the template (that is, the YAML header, R setup code chunk, text, R code chunk to produce a summary table, more text, and then another R code chunk). Go ahead and **knit** the template as is, and then compare the PowerPoint presentation output to the Markdown file that produced it. This exercise will help make even clearer how to work with Markdown as well as its potential applications. You can now use R Markdown to create your own presentations.

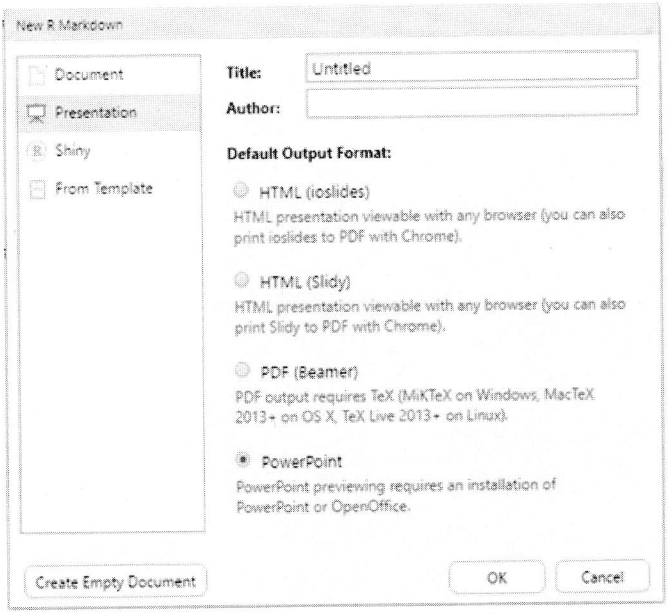

FIGURE 7.2. New R Markdown dialog box (presentation, PowerPoint).

KEY TAKEAWAYS

▲ R Markdown is a powerful tool for facilitating research reproducibility.

▲ It does this by integrating analysis code and reporting text.

▲ R Markdown can also facilitate creation of reports and presentations, and eases the task of updating them as necessary.

▲ Results of analyses and R objects or their elements can be integrated between blocks of text or inline with text.

EXERCISES

1. Using the data from Terrell (2021) on absences from class and scores on a final exam presented in Chapter 5, use R Markdown to create a Word document that provides descriptive statistics for the two variables, computes and tests the correlation coefficient, and displays a scatterplot with regression line (use *ggplot()* to create the scatterplot).

2. Repeat Exercise 1, but this time create an HTML document rather than a Word document as the output.

Functions

▼ Further consider the nature of R objects and functions.

▼ Understand the value of writing functions rather than copying, pasting, and editing blocks of code.

▼ Begin the journey of learning how to write functions.

In this chapter we dig a little deeper into R functions and begin to write our own. A key point to recall is that R works with objects. Objects contain some sort of information, for example, a data frame with raw data or with the output that resulted from some function. Functions instruct R regarding what to do with objects. We have seen this at every step of our way throughout this book. For example, consider again this code (which we also have seen in this book):

```
example_data <- read_excel("Example_Data.xlsx") %>%
  view()
```

This code uses the *read_excel()* function (from the *Readxl* package) to read an Excel file, assigns the data from the file (using the " <- "

assignment operator) to an object named *example_data*, and then uses the *view()* function to show the contents of the *example_data* object in a tab in RStudio's upper left-hand pane. The more familiar we become with R and with this notion using functions to operate on objects, the better able we are to make use of the power of the R software.

Writing a Function (Example 1)

We now turn to writing our own functions. By doing so, we can perform repetitive tasks with a reduced amount of code, which increases efficiency and reduces the opportunity for copy-and-paste errors. In addition, if updates are needed to the code, they can be done in fewer places.

Let's begin with the following function as an example. Functions contain a name, arguments, and body. This particular function is named *greetings*, which we create as a function by stating *function* on the right-hand side of the operator and providing the argument that will be passed to the function (here the argument is called *name*). Then, between the curly braces (" { } ") we have the body of the function which contains the code the function will execute. This function contains just one line of code so that it can be a simple illustration, though some functions may contain many more lines. Reading this line of code from the inside out, we see that it takes the argument passed to the function (*name*), uses the *sprintf()* function to return a formatted character vector containing the text and variables passed to it (*Greetings [name]*"), and then uses the *print()* function to display the result in the Console. We call the function in the form of *name of the function (and the argument passed to it)*. In our example below, our first function call is *greetings ("Person A")*, and in the Console we see that "*Greetings Person A*" has been returned. This is followed by two more calls, one for *Person B* and one for *Person C*. As powerful as this is, it becomes even more so as the code inside the function becomes longer or more complicated. Also, as we have seen before, we can assign the result of running a function to an object and then pass this new object on to other functions for their use. For example, this code from Chapter 6 uses the *lm()* function to create a linear model using the variables *score* and *absences* from the *go_to_class* data frame and assigns the results to the object named *go_to_class.model*. The *resid_panel()* function (from the *ggResidpanel* package) then operates on the *go_to_class.model* object to create the panel of residual diagnostic plots.

```
go_to_class.model <- lm(score ~ absenses, go_to_class)
resid_panel(go_to_class.model)
```

Go ahead and enter this code into an R script file and then run it.

```
# Create a function that says "Greetings!" to a person whose name
is passed to the function
greetings <- function(name)
{
  print(sprintf("Greetings Person %s!", name))
}


# Run the function for three individual names
greetings("A")
greetings("B")
greetings("C")
```

Running the code above produces the following output in the Console. As we can see, each function call passes the argument to the function, which then operates on it to produce a result. In this example, the first call—*greetings("A")*—returns the output *"Greetings Person A!"*

```
> # Create a function that says "Greetings!" to a person whose
name is passed to the function
> greetings <- function(name)
+ {
+   print(sprintf("Greetings Person %s!", name))
+ }
> # Run the function for three individual names
> greetings("A")
[1] "Greetings Person A!"
> greetings("B")
[1] "Greetings Person B!"
> greetings("C")
[1] "Greetings Person C!"
```

Writing a Function (Example 2)

Let's look at a second example. Suppose we want to create a new data frame that contains the means of selected variables in the *example_data*

data frame, including Outcome, Satisfaction, Effort_1, Effort_2, Effort_3, Effort_4, and Effort_5. The following code would accomplish this task:

```
# Compute means for seven variables in the example_data data frame
Mean_Outcome <- example_data %>%
  summarize(Mean = mean(Outcome))
Mean_Satisfaction <- example_data %>%
  summarize(Mean = mean(Satisfaction))
Mean_Effort_1 <- example_data %>%
  summarize(Mean = mean(Effort_1))
Mean_Effort_2 <- example_data %>%
  summarize(Mean = mean(Effort_2))
Mean_Effort_3 <- example_data %>%
  summarize(Mean = mean(Effort_3))
Mean_Effort_4 <- example_data %>%
  summarize(Mean = mean(Effort_4))
Mean_Effort_5 <- example_data %>%
  summarize(Mean = mean(Effort_5))

# Create data frame with the means just computed
Means <- data.frame(Mean_Outcome, Mean_Satisfaction,
                    Mean_Effort_1, Mean_Effort_2, Mean_Effort_3,
                    Mean_Effort_4, Mean_Effort_5)

# Look at the data
Means
```

Alternatively, we can select the variables of interest all at once and then use the *colMeans()* function to accomplish this task and compute the means, using the following code. Notice in particular that using the *colMeans()* function reduces the computational code to just three lines, far fewer than the code above (the difference in the number of lines of code would be even greater if we were computing the means of even more variables).

```
# Compute means for seven variables in the example_data data frame
#     using the colMeans() function
Means2 <- example_data %>%
  select(Outcome:Effort_5) %>%
  colMeans()

# Look at the data
Means2
```

Writing a Function (Example 3)

Let's now look at yet another example. Suppose we want to create a particular frequency table from a set of variables. The function below gives us the output that we want, which includes for each value of a variable the frequency, percentage, cumulative frequency, and cumulative percentage. The function is named *my_frequencies()*, takes the argument *var*, and performs the desired operations using the code inside the curly braces. We then call the function twice, once using a Tidyverse style and once using a Base R style (passing a different variable each time).

```
# Read data
example_data <- read_excel("Example_Data.xlsx") %>%
  print()


# Create a function to create a table with
#   frequency, percent, cumulative frequency, and cumulative percent
my_frequencies <- function(var)
{
  transform(table(var),
            Pct=round(prop.table(Freq)*100,digits=1),
            Cumulative_Freq=cumsum(Freq),
            Cumulative_Pct=cumsum(round(prop.table(Freq)*100,digits=1)))

}


# Call the function (Tidyverse style)
example_data %>%
  select(Effort_1) %>%
  my_frequencies()


# Call the function (Base R style)
my_frequencies(example_data$Effort_5)
```

The result, displayed in the Console, is as follows.

```
> # Create a function to create a table with
> #   frequency, percent, cumulative frequency, and cumulative percent
> my_frequencies <- function(var)
+ {
+   transform(table(var),
+             Pct=round(prop.table(Freq)*100,digits=1),
+             Cumulative_Freq=cumsum(Freq),
+             Cumulative_Pct=cumsum(round(prop.table(Freq)*100,digits=1)))
+
+ }
```

```
> # Call the function (Tidyverse style)
> example_data %>%
+   select(Effort_1) %>%
+   my_frequencies()
  var Freq Pct Cumulative_Freq Cumulative_Pct
1   1    3  30               3             30
2   2    4  40               7             70
3   3    2  20               9             90
4   4    1  10              10            100
> # Call the function (Base R style)
> my_frequencies(example_data$Effort_5)
  var Freq Pct Cumulative_Freq Cumulative_Pct
1   1    2  20               2             20
2   2    3  30               5             50
3   3    3  30               8             80
4   4    1  10               9             90
5   9    1  10              10            100
```

If we would like to call our function for a set of variables, rather than just a single variable, one way is to use the *map()* function (*map()* is a Tidyverse function); in Base R we could use the *lapply()* function). The following code provides an example of how we can use the *map()* function for this purpose. Note that the general format of the *map()* function is *map(variables, function)*; in the following code, we only need *map(function)* because the variables are being piped (" %>% ") through. The results from the *map()* function are collected in a data structure which R calls a *list*. In this example, the list contains five data frames, one for each of the tables created for the selected variables (that is, *Effort_1* through *Effort_5*). To help us understand the contents of the *set_of_tables* object, we can display it in the Console by entering its name (as for other objects), and we can use the *str()* function to display its structure in the Console. Go ahead and enter and run the following code.

```
# Use the map() function to apply a function to each element
#   of a list (or vector) and collect the results in a list
set_of_tables <- example_data %>%
  select(Effort_1:Effort_5) %>%
  map(my_frequencies)
# Display the object in the console
set_of_tables
```

This code produces the following output.

```
> # Use the map() function to apply a function to each element
> #   of a list (or vector) and collect the results in a list
> set_of_tables <- example_data %>%
+   select(Effort_1:Effort_5) %>%
+   map(my_frequencies)
> # Display the object in the console
> set_of_tables
$Effort_1
  var Freq Pct Cumulative_Freq Cumulative_Pct
1   1    3  30               3             30
2   2    4  40               7             70
3   3    2  20               9             90
4   4    1  10              10            100

$Effort_2
  var Freq Pct Cumulative_Freq Cumulative_Pct
1   1    2  20               2             20
2   2    5  50               7             70
3   3    2  20               9             90
4   4    1  10              10            100

$Effort_3
  var Freq Pct Cumulative_Freq Cumulative_Pct
1   1    2  20               2             20
2   2    1  10               3             30
3   3    6  60               9             90
4   4    1  10              10            100

$Effort_4
  var Freq Pct Cumulative_Freq Cumulative_Pct
1   1    2  20               2             20
2   2    1  10               3             30
3   3    5  50               8             80
4   4    1  10               9             90
5   5    1  10              10            100

$Effort_5
  var Freq Pct Cumulative_Freq Cumulative_Pct
1   1    2  20               2             20
2   2    3  30               5             50
3   3    3  30               8             80
4   4    1  10               9             90
5   9    1  10              10            100
```

We can also use the *str()* function to display the structure of this object:

```
# Display the structure of the object in the console
str(set_of_tables)
```

The line of code above displays in the Console the structure of the *set_of_tables* object.

```
> # Display the structure of the object in the console
> str(set_of_tables)
List of 5
 $ Effort_1:'data.frame':    4 obs. of  5 variables:
  ..$ var            : Factor w/ 4 levels "1","2","3","4": 1 2 3 4
  ..$ Freq           : int [1:4] 3 4 2 1
  ..$ Pct            : num [1:4] 30 40 20 10
  ..$ Cumulative_Freq: int [1:4] 3 7 9 10
  ..$ Cumulative_Pct : num [1:4] 30 70 90 100
 $ Effort_2:'data.frame':    4 obs. of  5 variables:
  ..$ var            : Factor w/ 4 levels "1","2","3","4": 1 2 3 4
  ..$ Freq           : int [1:4] 2 5 2 1
  ..$ Pct            : num [1:4] 20 50 20 10
  ..$ Cumulative_Freq: int [1:4] 2 7 9 10
  ..$ Cumulative_Pct : num [1:4] 20 70 90 100
 $ Effort_3:'data.frame':    4 obs. of  5 variables:
  ..$ var            : Factor w/ 4 levels "1","2","3","4": 1 2 3 4
  ..$ Freq           : int [1:4] 2 1 6 1
  ..$ Pct            : num [1:4] 20 10 60 10
  ..$ Cumulative_Freq: int [1:4] 2 3 9 10
  ..$ Cumulative_Pct : num [1:4] 20 30 90 100
 $ Effort_4:'data.frame':    5 obs. of  5 variables:
  ..$ var            : Factor w/ 5 levels "1","2","3","4",..: 1 2 3 4 5
  ..$ Freq           : int [1:5] 2 1 5 1 1
  ..$ Pct            : num [1:5] 20 10 50 10 10
  ..$ Cumulative_Freq: int [1:5] 2 3 8 9 10
  ..$ Cumulative_Pct : num [1:5] 20 30 80 90 100
 $ Effort_5:'data.frame':    5 obs. of  5 variables:
  ..$ var            : Factor w/ 5 levels "1","2","3","4",..: 1 2 3 4 5
  ..$ Freq           : int [1:5] 2 3 3 1 1
  ..$ Pct            : num [1:5] 20 30 30 10 10
  ..$ Cumulative_Freq: int [1:5] 2 5 8 9 10
  ..$ Cumulative_Pct : num [1:5] 20 50 80 90 100
```

As with other R objects, we can use functions to do things with elements of an object that was created by another function. For example, the following code uses the *flextable()* function to create a table from the *Satisfaction* data frame in the *set_of_tables* list.

Effort_1	Freq	Pct	Cumulative_Freq	Cumulative_Pct
1	3	30	3	30
2	4	40	7	70
3	2	20	9	90
4	1	10	10	100

FIGURE 8.1. Table Created from Dataframe in a List.

```
# Use the flextable() function on an item in the list
flextable(some_tables$Satisfaction) %>%
  set_header_labels(var = "Satisfaction")
```

This code produces the table shown in Figure 8.1.

The flextable package, including the *flextable()* function, provides a great deal of control over the table that is produced. The following code provides a glimpse into the many possibilities.

```
# Create the crosstabulation table
flextable(set_of_tables$Effort_1) %>%
  set_header_labels(var = "Effort ",
                    Freq = "Number",
                    Pct = "Percent",
                    Cumulative_Freq = "Cumulative Count",
                    Cumulative_Pct = "Cumulative Percent") %>%
  add_header_lines(values = "Frequency Distribution for Effort 1")
  autofit()
```

This code produces the table shown in Figure 8.2.

Frequency Distribution for Effort 5				
Effort 5	Number	Percent	Cumulative Count	Cumulative Percent
1	2	20	2	20
2	3	30	5	50
3	3	30	8	80
4	1	10	9	90
9	1	10	10	100

FIGURE 8.2. Table Created from Dataframe in a List, with Some Additional Formatting.

Do If—End If and Looping Structures

Since they are often part of the code we want when writing our own functions, let's now briefly review the *ifelse()* and *case_when()* functions. We used the *case_when()* function in Chapter 3 for recoding variables (noting that it is a general version of the *ifelse()* function), and we used the *ifelse()* function in Chapter 6 when we identified a bar to highlight in a graph. These functions are similar to *Do If—End If* type structures in other software. Running the following code will help us in our review. The first lines of code read the data and print selected variables. The next lines of code use the *ifelse()* function to recode the *Program* variable into a new variable named *Program_recoded* and then print selected variables. The last lines of code use the *case_when()* function to recode the *Program* variable into a new variable named *Program_recoded2* and then print selected variables.

```
# Read data
example_data <- read_excel("Example_Data.xlsx")

# Print selected variables from the example_data data frame
example_data %>%
  select(ID, Program) %>%
  print()

# Use ifelse() to recode Program into a new variable
example_data <- example_data %>%
  mutate(Program_recoded = if_else(Program == 1, 1, 0)) %>%
  select(ID, Program, Program_recoded) %>%
  print()

# Use case_when() to recode Program into another new variable
example_data <- example_data %>%
  mutate(Program_recoded2 = case_when(
     Program == 1 ~ 10,
     Program == 2 ~ 20)) %>%
  select(ID, Program, Program_recoded, Program_recoded2) %>%
  print()
```

R also has the ability to run structures similar to *Loop—End Loop* in other software, if that approach is the best way for us to solve a particular problem. For example, the following code creates a variable and then loops through the variable to square each value. Readers who wish to learn more about using loops in R may wish to see Wickham and Grolemund (2017) or Wickham (2014).

```
# Create variable, assign values, and show in the console
v1 <- c(1, 2, 3, 4, 5)
v1

# Square each value of the variable, and show in the console
for (i in 1:5) {
  v1[i] <-v1[i]^2
}
v1
```

However, it is generally nice to use functions where possible rather than writing our own looping structures. For example, we could write a loop to generate a vector of normally distributed random numbers, or instead we could use the *rnorm()* function. The following code generates a vector with 1,000 values, with a mean of zero and a standard deviation of one, and then it generates a histogram illustrating the distribution.

```
random_data <-  rnorm(1000, mean = 0, sd = 1)
hist(random_data)
```

We have now explored the fundamental ideas behind writing and using our own functions. I strongly encourage you to practice writing functions wherever it makes sense to do so, especially when you find yourself copying and pasting chunks of code that you then have to edit slightly so that they have different referents (for example, different variables). This will shorten your code, make it easier to update, and make it less prone to copy-and-paste errors.

KEY TAKEAWAYS

▲ R works with objects and functions.

▲ Objects contain some sort of information.

▲ Functions instruct R regarding what to do with objects.

▲ We can write our own functions, making our code shorter, easier to update, and less prone to copy-and-paste errors.

▲ Functions contain a name, receive arguments that are passed to it, and have a body that includes code written between curly braces.

EXERCISES

1. Modify the *my_frequencies* function so that it shows frequencies and percentages, but not the cumulative frequency and cumulative percentage.

2. Write a function that generates a vector of normally distributed random numbers, with a mean of zero and a standard deviation of one, so that the function call provides the number of values to be included in the vector; also have the function generate a histogram of the data. Call the function for values of 100, 1,000, and 10,000.

3. Modify the function from Exercise 2 so that the histogram is drawn using the *ggplot()* function rather than the *hist()* function (note that the vector needs to be converted to a data frame for use by the *ggplot()* function).

Next Steps

▼ **CHAPTER OBJECTIVES**

▼ Consider the next steps to take on the R journey.

▼ These steps include ways to find help, learn more about R and R programming,

find others in the R community, and learn more about statistics.

▼ Learn how to update R, R packages, and RStudio.

A s I mentioned at the beginning of the book, R is an extraordinarily powerful tool for statistical analysis and data visualization. It is remarkably vast in its capability, and this capability continues to increase as new packages are developed and made available. While this vastness is a great benefit, at times it can also be overwhelming, especially when the same task can be done in many different ways. In addition, RStudio is a remarkable tool with many capabilities beyond the ones mentioned here. In this chapter we think about the next steps on our R journey. These include:

• *Practice.* As with learning anything new, practice is key. The more R code we write and debug, and the more time we spend solving R puzzles, the more skilled we become. Keep in mind that distributing practice time can be more helpful than spending it in fewer sessions (that is, generally we can make more progress practicing 15 minutes per day than we can practicing an hour and a half once per week). Also, as mentioned early on, remember to breathe and to take breaks when needed; sometimes it is best just to step away from a task for a while, especially one that has become frustrating.

• **Continue learning.** In this chapter I will mention a variety of resources that are available for you to learn more about R, RStudio, and statistics. I encourage you to pursue them on an ongoing basis. Think about what tasks need to be accomplished, and seek out information about how to accomplish them. When encountering different ways of accomplishing a given task, think about which ones are most elegant, require the fewest lines of code, and work best given the workplace context and personal work style. The more familiar we become with R, the easier this is to do.

• **Think about the process of learning itself.** Along the way, pay attention to which resources are most helpful, ponder the difference between those that are helpful and those that are not, and also reflect on the processes by which R becomes ever more familiar as new learnings are applied. The more we practice, and the more developed our skills become, the more we have a sense of how to go about solving new puzzles using R and the easier it becomes to further extend and deepen our learning.

Finding Help

There are many sources of help available for you to figure out how to do things with R. Here are some examples. Practice using them so that you become ever better at finding the answers to your questions.

• **The help() function.** We can use the *help()* function to find out more about a package or function (alternatively, use a question mark followed by the name of the package or function). For example, entering either *help(ggplot2)* or *?ggplot2* reveals documentation about the *ggplot2* package in the Help tab in RStudio's lower right-hand pane. Similarly, *help(ggplot)* shows documentation about the *ggplot()* function, *help(aes)* shows documentation about the *aes()* function, and so on.

- **R package documentation.** In addition to being able to access documentation through the *help()* function, R packages are accompanied by documentation in .pdf form. We can find this documentation on the Comprehensive R Archive Network (CRAN) website (*https://cran.r-project.org*). On this website, we follow the *Packages* link and then click on the package of interest to learn about that package. In particular, we are interested in the package's *Reference Manual*, which we can download in .pdf format. As an example, the reference manual for the *rstatix* package is available at *https://cran.r-project.org/web/packages/rstatix/rstatix.pdf*. Spending time becoming familiar with the format of the reference manuals, as well as the content of the ones that are of interest, can be very useful in learning how to navigate the world of R.

- **Internet search.** It is possible to find quite a bit of information about R packages and functions through an Internet search. Depending on our search terms, the results may take us directly to R documentation on the CRAN website. We will also encounter many questions and answers provided by R users, and our particular question may have already been asked and answered. Just keep in mind that often R can accomplish a given task in more than one way, and it is good for each person to think for themselves about why some ways may be better than others for the particular code they are writing. For example, if one way to accomplish a task is to modify the data frame, and if another way to accomplish the same task is to use a function's options to work with the existing data frame, the latter approach will likely be preferable.

- **Cheatsheets.** RStudio has produced many very helpful cheatsheets. Several of these are available through the RStudio pull-down menus: **Help → Cheatsheets →**. Among them is the *RStuido IDE* cheatsheet, which we can use to expand and improve our skills for working in the RStudio integrated development environment. Additional cheatsheets are available on the RStudio website (*https://rstudio.com/resources/cheatsheets*). The RStudio **Help pull-down menu** shows other avenues for finding help as well.

- **Vignettes.** Many R packages provide vignettes to help us learn about the package. To see which of the packages that have been loaded in the current session have vignettes available, enter *vignette(all = FALSE)*; they will be listed in a tab that opens in the RStudio script pane. If we want to see all available vignettes, enter *vignette(all = TRUE)*. When we notice a vignette that we want to explore, enter *vignette()* with the name of the topic inside the parentheses and enclosed by quotation marks, for example, *vignette("forcats")*. The vignette will appear in the *RStuio* Help tab, and we can begin working through it.

The key point is that it is important develop an ability to learn new things, especially about those aspects of R that are relevant to our work and interests. As mentioned above, I encourage continual reflection on the process of learning, as we seek information and find answers to questions. This will aid our efforts to become ever more efficient and effective, and our R code becomes ever more improved. Considering, and applying, as appropriate, ideas such as those mentioned by Andersen (2016), may be very helpful. She notes the importance for learners to have aspiration, self-awareness, curiosity, and vulnerability (tolerating one's own mistakes while moving up the learning curve).

Learn More about R and R Programming

Many resources are available for learning about R and R programming. This availability is very helpful as R continues to develop, especially when there are major changes, such as further development within the Tidyverse (including the *ggplot2* package). Here are some suggestions for next steps in your R journey as you develop your programming skills and also keep up to date:

- *R for Data Science* by Hadley Wickham and Garrett Grolemund (2017) (*https://r4ds.had.co.nz*). This comprehensive book can help you build on your newly introduced skills.
- *ggplot2* by Hadley Wickham, Danielle Navarro, and Thomas Lin Pedersen (*https://ggplot2-book.org*). This book focuses on the grammar of graphics. The better you understand this grammar, the better able you will be to create the data visualizations that you imagine.

- The *R Markdown* website (*https://rmarkdown.rstudio.com*). Learn more about using RMarkdown on this website. Among the many resources available on this website is *R Markdown: The Definitive Guide* by Yihui Xie, J. J. Allaire, and Garrett Grolemund (*https://bookdown.org/yihui/rmarkdown*).

- The *Tidyverse* website (*www.tidyverse.org*). Learn more about the Tidyverse collection of packages on this website.

- The *Officeverse* website (*https://ardata-fr.github.io/officeverse*). Learn more about the Officeverse collection of packages on this website.

- *Hands-On Programming with R* by Garrett Grolemund (*https://rstudio-education.github.io/hopr*). This book will help you strengthen your R programming skills.

- *Efficient R Programming* by Colin Gillespie and Robin Lovelace (*https://csgillespie.github.io/efficientR*). This book will help increase the efficiency of both your R code and your workflow.

- *Advanced R* by Hadley Wickham (*https://adv-r.hadley.nz*). You can continue to deepen your R programming skills by studying this book.

- If you are interested in learning how to develop your own packages, the book *R Packages* by Hadley Wickham and Jenny Bryan will help you do so (*https://r-pkgs.org/intro.html*).

- *Happy Git and GitHub for the UseR* by Jenny Bryan, the STAT 545 TAs, and Jim Hester (*https://happygitwithr.com*). This book will help you learn to use the Git version control system and the GitHub website for sharing code. There is also a chapter on Git and GitHub in the *R Packages* book (*https://r-pkgs.org/git.html*).

Another way to learn more about using R is to follow the path forged by others. For example, in this book we used a data file that accompanied Hayes's (2022) *Introduction to Mediation, Moderation, and Conditional Process Analysis: A Regression-Based Approach*. The data file is available on the book's companion website,[1] which also includes a link to his PROCESS macro written for SPSS, SAS, and R.[2] Those

---

[1] *http://afhayes.com/introduction-to-mediation-moderation-and-conditional-process-analysis.html.*

[2] *www.processmacro.org/download.html.*

interested in these procedures may find a wealth of information here, including a macro already written for use in conducting these analyses in R.

As another example, an Internet search about how to use R to conduct latent variable analysis (for example, path analysis) might lead us to the *lavaan* package (*https://lavaan.ugent.be*). As described on the *lavaan* website, this package is intended for using "lavaan to estimate a large variety of multivariate statistical models, including path analysis, confirmatory factor analysis, structural equation modeling and growth curve models." The *lavaan* website provides considerable documentation, including a tutorial and links to several resources (including books and book chapters, videos, teaching materials, and other resources). The descriptions of some of these resources include links to R code; for example, on the Resources page there is a link to books, and on the Books page one of the resources is Brown's (2015) *Confirmatory Factor Analysis for Applied Research, Second Edition,* and another resource is Kline's (2015) *Principles and Practice of Structural Equation Modeling, Fourth Edition.* For both of these books, links are provided to accompanying R code, which you can download, study, and use.

As a third example, an Internet search for how to use R to conduct statistical power analysis may lead us to the *pwr* package. The description on the CRAN states that this package includes "Power analysis functions along the lines of Cohen (1988)." In addition to its reference manual, the *pwr* package also includes an extensive vignette. Working through the vignette provides a solid grounding in how to use the package to conduct power analyses.

These examples show that considerable documentation is available to help you learn how to use R to conduct your analyses. The key is to think about the information you want to find, to have a sense of where you might find it and the form in might be in, and to remain flexible in your thinking as you carry out your search. Once you find the information you are looking for, study it and try it out for your purposes. If you have found a package that will be useful, following up with the accompanying documentation and other support materials, especially working through the examples, may prove to be quite valuable. It can also be helpful to confirm your understanding of how to work with the package by first trying it out on a known problem (for instance, an example in a textbook) to confirm that you are obtaining the known answer to that problem, before conducting analysis on a new problem.

Community

Here are some ideas about where to find and connect with other R users:

- **R community.** By way of example, there is an *R for Data Science Online Learning Community* (*www.rfordatasci.com*), and many questions and answers may be found on *Stack Overflow* (*https://stackoverflow.com*).
- **R Conferences** (*www.r-project.org/conferences*). This website provides information about conferences that are supported and endorsed by the R Foundation.
- **RStudio events** (*https://rstudio.com/about/events*). This site provides information about RStudio events.
- **Local conferences and user groups.** There may be local conferences or user groups in your area, which you might find through an Internet search.

Learn More about Statistics

This book has assumed that you already have at least some familiarity with data analysis and statistics, or that you are concurrently gaining that familiarity. If you need resources in this area, here are a handful of suggestions.

- Terrell, S. R. (2021). *Statistics Translated: A Step-by-Step Guide to Analyzing and Interpreting Data* (2nd ed.). New York: Guilford Press.
- Field, A. (2016). *An Adventure in Statistics: The Reality Enigma.* Thousand Oaks, CA: Sage.

- Hayes, A. F. (2022). *Introduction to Mediation, Moderation, and Conditional Process Analysis: A Regression-Based Approach* (3rd ed.). New York: Guilford Press.
- Ismay, C., & Kim, A. Y. (2019). *Statistical Inference via Data Science: A ModernDive into R and the Tidyverse*. Boca Raton, FL: CRC Press. (*https://moderndive.com*)

Updating R, R Packages, and RStudio

New versions of R, R packages, and RStudio occasionally become available. It is worthwhile to keep your installation of R and RStudio up to date. Following is how you can do so.

Updating R

For Windows, we can use the *installr* package's *updateR()* function to update the R software. First, install the *installr* package (this can be done from within RStudio). When you are ready to call the *updateR()* function, do so from within the R graphical user interface Console rather than from within RStudio (see the *Working Directly in the R Console* section of Chapter 2). To update R, enter the following from within the R Console (see Figure 9.1):

```
> library(installr)
>updateR()
```

Updating R Packages

You can update packages from within RStudio. From the pull-down menus, select **Tools → Check for Package Updates . . .** A dialog box will appear showing you the packages that can be updated. Select the ones you want to update and then click the **Install Updates** button.

Updating RStudio

You can update RStudio from within the RStudio. From the pull-down menus, select **Help → Check for Updates.** A dialog box will appear

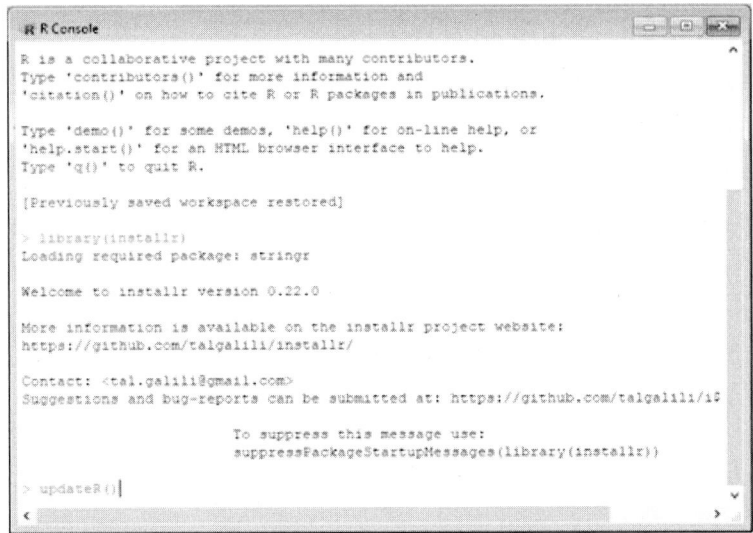

FIGURE 9.1. Updating R from within the R Console.

letting you know if an update is available. If so, click the *Quit and Download . . .* button to proceed. This will end your RStudio session and take you to the RStudio website where you can download and install the new version. If you are using the current version of RStudio, you will receive a message to that effect (see Figure 9.2).

⚠ KEY TAKEAWAYS

⚠ Remember to breathe and to take breaks when needed.

⚠ R is a vast resource—explore and learn.

⚠ Along the way, think about learning itself, so that you become an ever better learner.

⚠ Update your versions of R, R packages, and RStudio as needed.

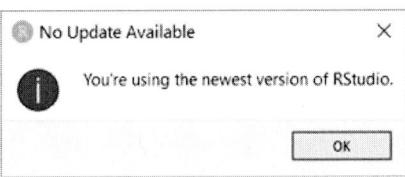

FIGURE 9.2. RStudio No Update Available dialog box.

EXERCISES

1. Obtain the *R Markdown cheatsheet*, locate the syntax for how to display text in bold, apply that syntax to some text in an R Markdown document, and knit the document to see the effect.

2. Review the vignette for *ggplot2* aesthetic specifications.

3. Review the *rstatix* package reference manual.

Conclusion

Up to this point we have covered a considerable amount of ground. We have installed R and RStudio, gained some familiarity with RStudio's layout, and begun to explore its capabilities. We used R to accomplish common data handling tasks and to perform fundamental statistical analyses. We have begun a study of the layered grammar of graphics and to think about how to apply these concepts as we go about creating data visualizations. We introduced RMarkdown, which integrates data analysis and reporting, and which can be a very useful tool in promoting reproducible research. We also began writing our own functions. Finally, we considered possible next steps on our R journey.

Throughout this book we have not only begun to learn how to use R and RStudio, but we have also given thought to our learning itself. R has such a vast collection of resources, and has so much flexibility in accomplishing tasks, that we need to be able to think about how to find the information we are looking for (for example, what R package has the tools we need) and then apply it to the task at hand. The better skilled we become at this process, the easier it becomes to find what we need and use it. This ease comes from practice, as well as from reflection on our practice regarding what works well and what does not work well for us, and making ongoing improvements. We have also encouraged flexibility in our thinking, in particular in being able to move between Base R and Tidyverse approaches to using R.

We have also recognized that learning new procedures, especially something like R, can at times be challenging or frustrating. At those times we might want to take a break and return to our project sometime later. After all, as challenging as it can be to solve a puzzle, finally reaching the solution can be quite rewarding.

Having worked through the material in this book, you now have a solid foundation upon which to further build your R skills. I encourage you to think about the many different ways you can apply these skills and to continue learning from the many available resources. In the process of developing and applying your skills, I encourage you to also have some fun.

R Data Structures

In this book we have encountered some types of R data structures, but we have not needed to delve into them. However, the more advanced your R skills become, the more it may be helpful for you to deepen your understanding. This appendix provides an awareness of this topic. Readers who want to explore these topics more thoroughly are referred to Wickham's *R for Data Science* and *Advanced R*, and *An Introduction to R* by Venables, Smith, and the R Core Team (available on the CRAN website[1]).

Data frame. A data frame contains variables, which can be of different types (for example, one variable can be numeric and another can be character). A **tibble** is a type of data frame. Throughout this book we have created data frames from two or more variables, for example, with code like this:

```
report_card <- data.frame(timing, motivation)
```

List. A list can contain components of different types. For example, it could contain a vector and a matrix, and even another list (thus lists are known as recursive rather than atomic).

Matrix. A matrix is a vector that also contains indicators for the number of rows and columns. An **array** is a multidimensional matrix, that is, a vector that contains indicators for the number of rows, columns, and layers.

Scalar. A vector of length one (i.e., it contains only one value).

Vector. The simplest R data structure is the vector. It is an object with an ordered set of values. Throughout this book we have created variables by assigning values, with code like this (in this example, *motivation* is an R vector):

```
motivation <- c(75, 68, 87, . . . 68, 67, 68)
```

---

[1] *https://cran.r-project.org/doc/manuals/r-release/R-intro.pdf*

Suggested Answers to Exercises

A s noted throughout this book, there is often more than one way to use R to solve an analytic problem. Thus, the code in this appendix provides one way to answer the exercises, but it is not necessarily the only way the exercises can be answered. Feel free to explore R's various capabilities as you work through the exercises.

Chapter 2

Exercise 3

```
view(diamonds)
```

Exercise 4

```
print(diamonds, n = 5)
```

Exercise 5

```
head(diamonds, n = 10)
```

Exercise 6

```
slice(diamonds, 3:7)
```

Exercise 7

```
tail(diamonds, n = 10)
```

Chapter 3

Exercise 1

```
diamonds2 <- diamonds %>%
    select(carat, cut, color, clarity, price)
  head(diamonds2)
```

Exercise 2

```
diamonds3 <- head(diamonds2, 10)
  diamonds3
```

Exercise 3

```
diamonds4 <- tail(diamonds2, 10)
  diamonds4
```

Exercise 4

```
diamonds5 <- bind_rows(diamonds3, diamonds4)
  diamonds5
```

Exercise 5

```
diamonds %>%
    group_by(color) %>%
    summarize(ave_price = mean(price)) %>%
    print()
```

Chapter 4

Exercise 1

```
# Create data frame
group <- c(1, 1, 1, 1, 1, 1, 1, 1, 1, 1, 1, 1, 1, 1, 1,
           2, 2, 2, 2, 2, 2, 2, 2, 2, 2, 2, 2, 2, 2, 2)
score  <- c(35, 32, 31, 33, 41, 35, 25, 31, 41, 40, 29, 61, 44, 31, 25,
            24, 42, 31, 25, 41, 32, 31, 31, 33, 31, 24, 20, 41, 25, 25)
sports <- data.frame(group, score)
# Make the variable group a factor
sports$group <- factor(sports$group,
                        levels = c(1 ,2),
                        labels = c("Plays Sports",
                                   "Does not Play Sports"))

# Look at the data
sports
```

```
# Summary statistics by group
sports %>%
  group_by(group) %>%
  get_summary_stats(score,
    show = c("n", "min", "max", "median", "mean", "sd"))
```

Exercise 2

```
#  Levene's test
sports %>%
  levene_test(score ~ group, center = mean)

#  t-test for independent samples (equal variances assumed, based on
results of Levene's test)
sports %>%
  t_test(score ~ group, var.equal = TRUE, detailed = TRUE,
  alternative = "less")
```

Plays sports: mean = 35.6, SD = 9.05
Does not play sports: mean = 30.4, SD = 6.80
Levene's test = .466, p = .501
t = 1.78, df = 28, p = .957

Exercise 3

```
# Create data frame
pill <- c(1, 1, 1, 1, 1,
          2, 2, 2, 2, 2,
          3, 3, 3, 3, 3)
minutes <- c(8, 8, 7, 3, 5,
             6, 6, 5, 4, 2,
             8, 9, 2, 8, 2)
pill <- as.factor(pill)
relief  <- data.frame(pill, minutes)
# Summary statistics overall
relief %>%
  get_summary_stats(minutes,
               show = c("n", "min", "max", "median", "mean", "sd"))
# Summary statistics by group
relief %>%
  group_by(pill) %>%
  get_summary_stats(minutes,
               show = c("n", "min", "max", "median", "mean", "sd"))

# Oneway ANOVA
relief %>%
  anova_test(minutes ~ pill, detailed = TRUE)
```

Between groups: sum of squares = 6.933, $df = 2$, mean square = 3.467
Within groups: sum of squares = 78.800, $df = 12$, mean square = 6.567
Total: sum of squares = 85.733, $df = 14$
$F = .528$
$p = .603$

Exercise 4

```
# Create data table
prereq <- as.table(
  rbind(c(24, 10, 7, 6, 7), c(10, 15, 13, 11, 12))
)
dimnames(prereq) <- list(
  Major = c("Psychology", "Other"),
  Grade = c("A", "B", "C", "D", "F")
)


# Look at the data frame
prereq

# Obtain the chi-square test statistic and probability (Option 1)
prereq %>%
  chisq.test()

# Obtain the chi-square test statistic and probability (Option 2)
prereq %>%
  chisq_test()

# Obtain the chi-square details
prereq %>%
  chisq_test() %>%
  chisq_descriptives() %>%
  flextable()
```

chi-square = 10.966
$p = .027$

Chapter 5

Exercise 1

```
# Create the data frame
year <- c(1, 2, 3, 4, 5, 6, 7, 8, 9, 10)
tuition <- c(32, 38, 41, 42, 50, 60, 57, 70, 80, 100)
resignations <- c(20, 25, 28, 25, 30, 32, 40, 45, 45, 90)
t_r  <- data.frame(year, tuition, resignations)

# Look at the data frame in the Console
t_r
```

```
# Create the scatterplot
plot(t_r$tuition, t_r$resignations)

# Improve the scatterplot
plot(t_r$tuition, t_r$resignations,
     xlim = c(0, 100),
     ylim = c(0, 100),
     pch = 16,
     col = "black",
     main = "Scatterplot of Tuition and Resignations",
     xlab = "Tuition Paid",
     ylab = "Resignations")
```

Pearson's correlation $= 0.926$

Exercise 2

```
abline(lm(resignations ~ tuition, t_r))
```

Exercise 3

```
# Regression analysis
lm(resignations ~ tuition, t_r) %>%
  summary()

# Regression analysis using the moderndive package
library(moderndive)
lm(resignations ~ tuition, t_r) %>%
  get_regression_table()
lm(resignations ~ tuition, t_r) %>%
  get_regression_summaries()
lm(resignations ~ tuition, t_r) %>%
  get_regression_points()
```

Coefficients: intercept $= -12.09, p = 0.153$; tuition $= .88, p < .001$
$F = 47.99$ on 1 an 8 df
$p < .001$

Chapter 6

Exercise 1

```
favorites %>%
  mutate(highlight = ifelse(foods == "Food 3",
                            "Highlighted", "Normal")) %>%
  ggplot(mapping = aes(x = reorder(foods, people),
                       y = people,
                       fill = highlight)) +
```

```
geom_bar(stat = "identity", width = .5) +
scale_fill_manual(values = c("Highlighted" = "blue2", "Normal" = "green3")) +
geom_text(label = favorites$people, hjust = -0.5) +
ylim(0, 20) +
labs(title = "Favorite Foods",
     x = "Foods",
     y = "Number of People") +
theme_bw() +
theme(legend.position = "none") +
coord_flip()
```

Exercise 2

As in Exercise 1 above, but with colors of your choice in the *scale_fill_manual()* function

Exercise 3

```
math_study %>%
  ggplot(aes(x = type, y = grade)) +
  geom_boxplot() +
  ylim(50, 100) +
  labs(title = "Effect of Three Instructional Methods on Math Achievement",
       x = "Type of Instruction",
       y = "Grade") +
  theme_gray()
```

Exercise 4

```
t_r %>%
  ggplot(aes(x = tuition, y = resignations)) +
  geom_point() +
  xlim(0, 100) +
  ylim(0, 100) +
  geom_smooth(method = "lm", se = FALSE, color = "black") +
  labs(title = "Scatterplot of Tuition and Resignations",
       x = "Tuition Paid (Thousands)", y = "Resignations") +
  theme_classic()
```

Chapter 7

Exercise 1

```
---
title: "Absences and Final Exam Scores"
output: word_document
---
```

```
```{r setup, include=FALSE}
knitr::opts_chunk$set(echo = FALSE)

# Load packages
library(tidyverse)
library(rstatix)
library(flextable)

# Set options so that scientific notation isn't used
# Run with this line commented out to use scientific notation
#    (i.e., reporting the p value for the correlation coefficient)
options(scipen = 999)

```

Introduction
```

Example from Terrell (2021) looking at the correlation between absences in class and score on a final exam.

```
```{r, echo = FALSE}

# Create the data frame
absences <- c(1, 2, 4, 5, 6, 4, 6, 7, 2, 7,
              7, 9, 11, 2, 1, 12, 6, 7, 2,3)
score <- c(100, 95, 90, 90, 80, 85, 82, 80, 97, 77,
           70, 90, 55, 94, 90, 70, 80, 80, 93, 88)
go_to_class <- data.frame(absences, score)

# Look at the data frame
#go_to_class

# Create object with descriptive statistics results
desc_results <- go_to_class %>%
  get_summary_stats(show = c("n", "min", "max", "mean", "sd"))
#print(desc_results)

```

Results

As shown in the table below:

* The results are based on the `r nrow(go_to_class)` cases in our data frame.

* The mean number of absences was `r desc_results %>%
  filter(variable == "absences") %>%
  select(mean)` with a standard deviation of `r desc_results %>%
  filter(variable == "absences") %>%
  select(sd) %>%
  mutate(sd = round(sd, digits = 1))`.
```

```
* The mean final exam score was `r desc_results %>%
   filter(variable == "score") %>%
   select(mean)` with a standard deviation of `r desc_results %>%
   filter(variable == "score") %>%
   select(sd) %>%
   mutate(sd = round(sd, digits = 1))`.


```{r, echo = FALSE}

# Descriptive statistics
go_to_class %>%
   get_summary_stats(show = c("n", "min", "max", "mean", "sd")) %>%
   flextable() %>%
   autofit()
```


The correlation between number of absences and final exam score was `r
go_to_class %>%
   cor_test(absences, score) %>%
   select(cor)` (p = `r go_to_class %>% cor_test(absences, score) %>% s
elect(p)`). The data are displayed in the following graph.

```{r, echo = FALSE, message = FALSE}

# Draw the graph
go_to_class %>%
   ggplot(aes(x = score, y =  absences)) +
   geom_point() +
   xlim(50, 100) +
   ylim(0, 15) +
   geom_smooth(method = "lm", se = FALSE, color = "black") +
   labs(title = "Scatterplot of Absences and Final Exam Score",
        x = "Score", y = "Absences") +
   theme_classic()
```
```

Exercise 2

In the YAML for Exercise 1 above change

```
output: word_document
```

to

```
output: html_document
```

Chapter 8

Exercise 1

```
# Create a function to create a table with frequency and percentages
my_frequencies2 <- function(var)
{
  transform(table(var),
            Pct=round(prop.table(Freq)*100,digits=1))


}

# Run the my_frequencies function (Tidyverse style)
example_data %>%
  select(Effort_1) %>%
  my_frequencies2()
```

Exercise 2

```
# Function to create a vector of normally distributed random
# numbers and draw a histogram of the data
my_random <- function(var)
{
  random_data  <-  rnorm((var), mean = 0, sd = 1)
  hist(random_data)
}

# Call the function
my_random(100)
my_random(1000)
my_random(10000)
```

Exercise 3

```
# Function to create a vector of normally distributed random
# numbers and draw a histogram of the data using ggplot()
my_random2 <- function(var)
{
  random_data2  <-  rnorm(10000, mean = 0, sd = 1)
  random_data2 <- data.frame(random_data2)
  random_data2 %>%
    ggplot(mapping = aes(x = random_data2)) +
    geom_histogram(color = "gray75")
}

# Call the function
my_random2(100)
my_random2(1000)
my_random2(10000)
```

Chapter 9

Exercise 1

The R Markdown cheatsheet (and other cheatsheets) are available on the RStudio website (*www.rstudio.com/resources/cheatsheets*). You can also access it through RStudio (**Help → Cheatsheets → R Markdown Cheatsheet**). Surrounding text in an R Markdown file with double asterisks (for example, " ** *text* ** ") causes that text to be rendered in bold.

Exercise 2

Use the following code to see what vignettes are available for the *ggplot2* package (if you have the package installed, otherwise set (all = TRUE) or install the package).

```
vignette(all = FALSE)
```

Scroll down the list of vignettes and notice that there is a one named *ggplot2-specs* that contains information about aesthetic specifications. Run the following code to show the vignette:

```
vignette("ggplot2-specs")
```

Exercise 3

The *rstatix* package reference manual is available at *https://cran.r-project.org/web/packages/rstatix/rstatix.pdf*.

References

Anderson, E. (2016). Learning to learn. *Harvard Business Review, 94*(3), 98-101.

Bollen, K., Cacioppo, J. T., Kaplan, R. M., Krosnick, J. A., & Olds, J. L. (2015). *Social, Behavioral, and Economic Sciences Perspectives on Robust and Reliable Science*. Report of the Subcommittee on Replicability in Science Advisory Committee to the National Science Foundation Directorate for Social, Behavioral, and Economic Sciences. Retrieved from *www.nsf.gov/sbe/AC_Materials/SBE_Robust_and_Reliable_Research_Report.pdf*.

Brown, T. (2015). *Confirmatory Factor Analysis for Applied Research* (2nd ed.). New York: Guilford Press.

Bryan, J., the STAT 545 TAs, & Hester, J. (n.d.). *Happy Git and GitHub for the UseR*. Retrieved from *https://happygitwithr.com*.

Cohen, J. (1988). *Statistical Power Analysis for the Behavioral Sciences* (2nd ed.). Mahwah, NJ: Erlbaum.

Field, A. (2016). *An Adventure in Statistics: The Reality Enigma*. Thousand Oaks, CA: SAGE.

Gillespie, C., & Lovelace, R. (2017). *Efficient R Programming*. Sebastopol, CA: O'Reilly Media. Online at *https://csgillespie.github.io/efficientR*.

Grolemund, G. (2014). *Hands-On Programming with R*. Sebastopol, CA: O'Reilly Media. Online at *https://rstudio-education.github.io/hopr*.

Hayes, A. F. (2022). *Introduction to Mediation, Moderation, and Conditional Process Analysis: A Regression-Based Approach* (3rd ed.). New York: Guilford Press.

Ismay, C., & Kim, A. Y. (2019). *Statistical Inference via Data Science: A Modern Dive into R and the Tidyverse*. London: Chapman & Hall. Online at *https://moderndive.com/*

Kline, R. B. (2015). *Principles and Practice of Structural Equation Modeling* (4th ed.). New York: Guilford Press.

National Academies of Sciences, Engineering, and Medicine. (2019). *Reproducibility and Replicability in Science.* Washington, DC: National Academies Press.

R Core Team. (2021). R: A Language and Environment for Statistical Computing [Software]. Vienna, Austria: R Foundation for Statistical Computing. *https://www.R-project.org/*

Schochet, P. Z. (2009). An approach for addressing the multiple testing problem in social policy impact evaluations. *Evaluation Review, 33*(6), 539–567.

Terrell, S. R. (2021). *Statistics Translated: A Step-by-Step Guide to Analyzing and Interpreting Data* (2nd ed.). New York: Guilford Press.

Venables, W. N., Smith, D. M., and the R Core Team. An Introduction to R. Notes on R: A Programming Environment for Data Analysis and Graphics Version 4.1.2 (2021-11-01) Online at *https://cran.r-project.org/doc/manuals/r-release/R-intro.pdf.*

Wasserstein, R. L., & Lazar, N. A. (2016). The ASA statement on *p*-values: Context, process, and purpose. *The American Statistician, 70*(2), 129–133.

Wasserstein, R. L., Schirm, A. L., & Lazar, N. A. (2019). Moving to a world beyond "*p* < 0.05." *The American Statistician, 73*(Suppl. 1), 1–19.

Wickham, H. (2010). A layered grammar of graphics, *Journal of Computational and Graphical Statistics, 19*(1), 3–28.

Wickham, H. (2014). *Advanced R.* Boca Raton, FL: CRC Press. Online at *https://adv-r.hadley.nz.*

Wickham, H., & Bryan, J. (2015). *R Packages.* Sebastopol, CA: O'Reilly Media. Online at *https://r-pkgs.org/index.html.*

Wickham, H., & Grolemund, G. (2017). *R for Data Science.* Sebastopol, CA: O'Reilly Media. Online at *https://r4ds.had.co.nz.*

Wickham, H., Navarro, D., & Pedersen, T. L. (2016). *ggplot2: Elegant Graphics for Data Analysis* (3rd ed.) (work in progress). Online at *https://ggplot2-book.org.*

Xie, Y., Allaire, J. J., & Grolemund, G. (2018). *R Markdown: The Definitive Guide.* Boca Raton, FL: CRC Press. Online at *https://bookdown.org/yihui/rmarkdown.*

Index

About the Author

Eric L. Einspruch, PhD, is an independent researcher and program evaluator based in Oregon. Since the 1980s, he has led, managed, and conducted a wide variety of studies to inform policy development and program improvement. As an adjunct professor at Portland State University, OHSU-PSU School of Public Health, and elsewhere, he has taught graduate, undergraduate, and certificate courses. He has taught in the areas of program evaluation, research methods, data analysis, and emergency management and community resilience. Dr. Einspruch's work has appeared in peer-reviewed journal articles, books, and book chapters. He is the recipient of Portland State University's inaugural Adjunct Excellence Award for Research (2017), and, with his coauthors, received the Helen Tobin Writers' Award (2012) for an article published in the *Journal for Nurses in Staff Development.* Dr. Einspruch was among the organizers of the Oregon Program Evaluators Network, a local affiliate of the American Evaluation Association, and served as its charter secretary during its first 2 years and as its fifth president. He is an avid learner of new ideas, information, and skills who enjoys helping others advance their own learning. His website is *www.eleconsulting.com.*